More from

ACE BAKERY

More from

ACE BAKERY

RECIPES FOR AND WITH BREAD

by

Linda Haynes

whitecap

Whitecap Books

Edited by Nicole de Montbrun
Proofread by Joan Tetrault
Editorial Advisor to Linda Haynes: Rosalind Whelan
Cover by Five Seventeen
Interior by Michelle Mayne and Five Seventeen
Photography by Douglas Bradshaw Photography
Food Styling by Claire Stubbs

LIBRARY AND ARCHIVES CANADA CATALOGUING IN PUBLICATION

Haynes, Linda, 1951-
    More from ACE Bakery / Linda Haynes.

    Includes index.
    ISBN 1-55285-808-1
    ISBN 978-1-55285-808-0

    1. Cookery. 2. Cookery (Bread) I. Title.

TX769.H393 2006   641.5   C2006-900702-0

The publisher acknowledges the financial support of the Government of Canada through the Book Publishing Industry Development Program (BPIDP) and the Province of British Columbia through the Book Publishing Tax Credit.

Printed in Canada

To my favourite dinner companions —
Martin, Devin, and Luke

Acknowledgements

Many thanks to

Anya Oberdorf who worked with me for 5 months developing, testing and retesting recipes;

My mother, who continues to give me refresher courses in the kitchen;

My brother Phil who always inspires us in the development of the ACE brand;

Seanna, Ted, Sierra, John, Shauna, Pyper, Finn, Lindsey and Jim—my expanding family whose encouragement gets me up in the morning;

Darcy for constantly being a thoughtful booster;

Emily for her research, recipe testing and honest feedback;

Brendan for being a great pinch hitter;

Marcus Mariathas, Tom Vas, Abdellah Chadli and Joe Laface for all the hours spent helping me adapt bread recipes for the home;

My colleagues at ACE whose professionalism and enthusiasm make it a joy to go to work;

Rosalind Whelan who once again patiently provided her publishing experience to ensure this book reads the way I intended;

Robert McCullough, publisher, whose friendship has continued to be a bright light and Five Seventeen, art director, whose terrific design sense shines through on every page;

Doug Bradshaw and Claire Stubbs, the superbly talented photographer/stylist team, for their creative and beautiful shots;

Hyacinth Anderson and Annette Drean for their years of support in all I do, especially in the kitchen;

Suzanne Fitzgerald for keeping my business and personal life on track during the writing of this book;

Amos Bomze, owner of Toronto's wonderful butcher shop, Olliffe, for his generosity and good advice;

and Janice Daciuk, whose exacting testing will hopefully make the recipes foolproof.

Preface

When publisher Robert McCullough approached me to write a second cookbook, I was flattered, but apprehensive. ACE Bakery was almost 13 years old and we had expanded from a Toronto-based bakery to selling bread across most of Canada, into the northern and Midwest U.S. and the Bahamas. I wasn't sure I had to time to write another cookbook that I would be as happy with as the first one. But Robert's sweet-talking ways are hard to resist. It didn't take me long to sign the contract.

This is a continuation of *The ACE Bakery Cookbook*. Some recipes are made at our Fresh Bread Store and Café; others were created for breakfast, lunch and dinner with family and friends. As with the first book, all the recipes have been tested by home cooks, with the more complicated ones being retested by a professional recipe tester.

I hope you will enjoy making and sharing these recipes with your family and friends as much as I have with mine.

Linda

"Laughter is brightest where food is best."
—Irish proverb

Contents

"To bring a person into your house is to take charge of his happiness for as long as he is under your roof."

— Anthelme Brillat-Savarin

Breads—Yeasted and Quick

"Bread is the king of the table and all else is merely the court that surrounds the king. The countries are the soup, the meat, the vegetables, the salad ... but bread is king."
—Louis Bromfield

Baking 101

1. Measure all your ingredients first.

2. Whenever possible, use a kitchen scale to measure ingredients, as weight measurements will be more accurate than volume, such as cups or millilitres. Different flours, even different salts, will weigh the same although their volumes will be different. A ton of feathers does weigh the same as a ton of stone. For example, ½ ounce (14 g) of kosher salt will measure 3½ teaspoons (17.5 mL), while the equivalent weight in table salt will measure 2 teaspoons (10 mL). For the bread recipes in this first section, I have listed the dry ingredients by weight rather than volume. In the past, whenever I've relied on cups, tablespoons, or millilitres, the final product has not turned out as well as it should have. But because household scales are not precise enough to weigh small quantities, I have converted those to volume measurements.

3. Since you will be working in fits and starts, begin by making a schedule of when each step should take place before you even start the recipe. Leave it beside your bowl or pan.

4. For the bread recipes in this book I have used unbleached hard flour, traditional dry yeast, unsalted butter, and kosher or sea salt.

5. You will need a standing mixer with a dough hook, a low-temperature thermometer (some meat thermometers will do), a spray bottle, an oven thermometer, and patience.

6. Always cover your dough after each procedure to prevent it from forming a dry crust that will inhibit rising.

7. Spraying hot water into the oven just before baking will ensure what bakers call a good spring (accelerated rise) and a crisp crust.

8. In humid weather you will need slightly less liquid, and in dry weather you will need slightly more.

9. The optimum temperature for your finished dough before it goes into the oven should be about 74° to 75°F (23° to 24°C).

10. Your room temperature and water temperature will affect how quickly your starter or dough will rise. These recipes were tested in a home kitchen where the temperature ranged from 70° to 74°F (21° to 23°C). Dough will rise faster in a warmer kitchen.

Zucchini, Carrot and Gruyère Loaf

MAKES 3 SMALL LOAVES

Anya Oberdorf, my assistant on this book, created these loaves (photo page 83) when we had a surplus of carrots and zucchini in the kitchen. This isn't a yeasted dough so it's ready to eat in just over 90 minutes. We like to spread slices of the loaf with herbed cream cheese and serve it with a bowl of Tomato, Ginger and Orange Soup (see page 81).

½ cup (120 mL) olive oil
4 large eggs
3 cups (720 mL) all-purpose flour
2 tsp. (10 mL) baking powder
2 tsp. (10 mL) baking soda
2 light tsp. (10 mL) kosher salt
⅔ cup (160 mL) peeled and coarsely grated carrot (1 to 2 medium carrots)

1⅓ cups (320 mL) unpeeled, seeded, and coarsely grated zucchini (about 1 to 2 medium zucchini)
1 cup (240 mL) coarsely grated Gruyère, about 6 oz. (170 g)
1 Tbsp. (15 mL) finely chopped fresh sage
1 tsp. (5 mL) finely chopped fresh thyme
1 egg white

Preheat the oven to 350°F (175°C).

In a small bowl, whisk together the olive oil and the whole eggs.

In a mixing bowl large enough to hold all of the ingredients, combine 2½ cups (600 mL) flour, baking powder, baking soda, and salt. Make a well in the center of the dry ingredients and pour in the egg mixture. Using a fork, slowly begin incorporating the flour from the edges of the well into the egg mixture.

Once the flour and eggs are well combined, add the carrots, zucchini, cheese, and herbs and gently knead into the dough with your hands. The dough will become fairly wet again.

Spread the remaining ½ cup (120 mL) flour on a flat surface and turn the dough onto it. Knead to incorporate all of the flour into the dough. Use the traditional push-pull method, allowing your palms to push the dough along the surface away from you and then pull it back over itself.

Grease three loaf pans, approximately 2½ × 6 × 3½ inches (6.2 × 15 × 8.7 cm) with a little butter and dust with flour.

Divide the dough into 3 pieces and place in the pans. In a small bowl, lightly whisk the egg white and brush sparingly onto the top of the loaves. Bake for 35 to 40 minutes or until a skewer comes out clean. Remove from the oven and let cool for 10 minutes before removing from the pans. Allow to cool completely before slicing.

Strawberry Mint Jam p. 51

Challah

MAKES ONE BRAIDED LOAF

If you're in the mood to impress your family and friends, this recipe will do the trick. When you bring your stunning-looking and delicious-tasting creation to the table, only you will know how little effort it took to get it there. Because this challah has one short fermentation period followed by a short proofing period, it will be ready to serve in much less time than the other bread recipes in this book. If you make the starter the night before, your challah will be out of the oven in just under three hours. Don't be intimidated by the braiding. You will find these instructions very easy to follow.

PÂTE FERMENTÉE (STARTER)
⅓ cup + 2 tsp. (90 mL) cool water
   at 65°F (18°C)
¼ tsp. (1.2 mL) traditional dry yeast
4½ oz. (128 g) unbleached hard white flour
½ tsp. (2.5 mL) fine sea salt
vegetable oil to grease a bowl

FINAL DOUGH
¾ cup + 2 Tbsp. + 2 tsp. (220 mL) cool water
   at 65°F (18°C)
1½ tsp. (7.5 mL) traditional dry yeast
10 ½ oz. (400 g) unbleached hard white flour
3½ oz. (100 g) semolina flour
4 large egg yolks
⅓ cup (80 mL) wildflower or acacia honey
2 Tbsp. (30 mL) softened unsalted butter
1½ tsp (7.5 mL) fine sea salt
3⅓ oz. (90 g) starter
vegetable oil to grease a bowl
1 egg yolk + 2 tsp. (10 mL) water
sesame seeds for topping (optional)

STARTER

Place the water, yeast, unbleached flour, and sea salt into the mixing bowl of a standing mixer in the order listed. Stir with a spatula for 1 minute to mix the ingredients together.

Cover the mixing bowl with a kitchen towel and let the starter rest for 15 minutes. Lightly grease a bowl large enough to allow the starter to expand to double its mass.

Attach the dough hook to the mixer and mix the dough at slow (speed #2) for 3 minutes.

Place the dough in the oiled bowl and cover with plastic wrap. Let it ferment at room temperature in a draft-free area for about 5 hours or until it has almost doubled in bulk.

Alternatively, as soon as the dough is in the oiled bowl and covered, refrigerate it for 10 to 12 hours. Remove from the refrigerator and allow the covered starter to ferment at room temperature, in a draft-free area for about 1 hour or until it reaches 55° to 61°F (12° to 16°C). Once it does, you can proceed with the recipe.

continued ...

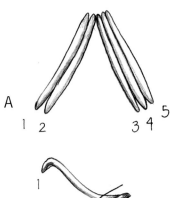

A

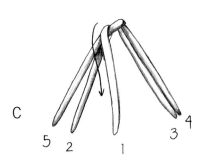

B

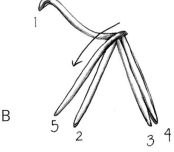

C

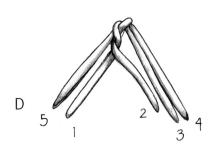

D

FINAL DOUGH

Place the cool water, yeast, flour, semolina flour, egg yolks, honey, butter, sea salt, and starter into the bowl of a standing mixer and stir with a spatula for 1 minute to mix the ingredients together. Attach the dough hook and mix the dough at "stir" speed for 2 minutes, followed by 2 minutes at slow (speed #2) and 4 minutes at fast (speed #4).

Lightly oil the interior of a bowl large enough to allow the dough to expand by about 50 percent.

Move the dough to the oiled bowl, turning it over so that it is lightly coated in oil. Cover with a kitchen towel and place in a draft-free area. The dough should increase in size by about 50 percent in 1 hour.

Once it has expanded, divide the dough into 5 pieces of equal weight. Roll each piece into a strand approximately 15 inches (38 cm) long. Slightly taper all the ends.

This method for braiding bread comes from *Bread: A Bakers Book of Techniques and Recipes*:

Place the strands vertically on a lightly floured surface. Move two strands to the left and three to the right. Arrange the strands so that the tips farthest from you touch, with the tips nearest to you spreading out to form an inverted V, keeping two strands to the left and three to the right (Illustration A).

Lift strands 1 and 5. Bring strand 5 over and to the outside of strand 2 (Illustration B).

Place strand 1 on the inside of strand 2 (Illustration C).

Twist strand 2 over strand 1. Strand 1 should be parallel to strand 5 and strand 2 should be parallel to strand 3 (Illustration D).

Bring strand 4 over strands 1 and 2. It should lie between strands 1 and 5 (Illustration E).

Move strand 5 between strands 1 and 2 (Illustration F).

Twist strand 1 over strand 5, bringing strand 5 beside strand 4 and strand 1 beside strand 2 (Illustration G). The braid should be fairly tight. Arrange the remaining length of the strands with two to the left and three to the right.

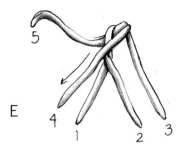

E

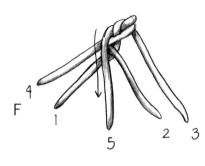

F

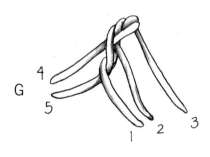

G

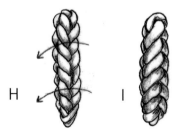

H   I

Repeat this pattern, starting at Illustration B, until all the dough is used. Tuck the ends together at the end of the braid (Illustration H).

The loaf will be lying on its side. Roll it to the left so that the right side of the loaf is now on top. It will have parallel strands of dough running at an angle down the length of the dough (Illustration H). Tuck the other strands of the dough together and using both hands, gently arrange the dough into an even loaf.

If you find the braiding instructions too daunting, divide the dough in half and form into 2 boules. (See Cook's Tip, page 23.)

In a small bowl, whisk the egg yolk and water together to make an egg wash. Lightly brush a very small amount of the wash over the challah. You will be brushing it again after the next rise.

Gently transfer the braided dough to a lightly oiled baking tray. Cover with a kitchen towel or lightly greased plastic wrap and let the loaf rest for 45 minutes in a draft-free area at room temperature. It should increase in size by about 50 percent.

Meanwhile, preheat the oven to 365°F (185°C).

Remove the towel and once more lightly brush the surface of the challah with the egg wash. (If you use too much wash, the challah will look burned after baking.) Sprinkle with sesame seeds (optional). Bake the bread on the middle rack for 30 minutes.

Remove the bread from the oven. You may find the bread sticks to the tray where the egg wash has run down the side of the bread. Use a spatula to free it. To test if the bread is baked, tap your fingertips on the bottom of the loaf. If it is ready, it will sound hollow. If not, return the bread to the oven for another few minutes. Put the challah on a rack to cool and let sit for 2 hours before slicing.

COOK'S TIP

Store challah in a paper or cloth bag at room temperature. Don't refrigerate or store bread in a plastic bag. Refrigeration will draw out the moisture from the bread and a plastic bag will soften the crust. Challah freezes well and leftover bread makes delicious French toast or bread pudding.

Cheddar Roll Cluster

MAKES 9 TO 12 ROLLS

ACE Cheese Twists, which we sell in bundles of four, have a cult following. There is a lot of complicated handwork involved in the process and a high risk for error. Rolling 9 or 12 equal pieces of dough into balls, and joining them together to make a pretty cluster, is an easier task and the taste doesn't suffer a bit. You will want to use cheese with a bit of a zing, but not so strong that it overpowers the loaf. I have found that 2-year-old cheddar from some dairies has the same bite as a 5-year-old from another cheese maker. I leave the choice to you.

Once your starter is made you will have two mixing sessions of a few minutes each, and one short resting period of 15 minutes. Both the fermentation and proofing times range from 45 minutes to 1 hour. You can also make two boules (rounds) with this amount of dough. For instructions on forming them, see the Cook's Tip at the end of the recipe.

PÂTE FERMENTÉE (STARTER)

¼ tsp. (1.2 mL) traditional dry yeast
1 Tbsp. + 1½ tsp. (22.5 mL) lukewarm water at 75° to 90°F (24° to 32°C)
⅓ cup (80 mL) cool water at 65°F (18°C)
4½ oz. (128 g) unbleached white hard flour
½ tsp. (2.5 mL) kosher or fine sea salt
vegetable oil to grease a bowl

FINAL DOUGH

1⅓ cups + 1 Tbsp. (335 mL) cool water at 65°F (18°C)
1 tsp. (5 mL) traditional dry yeast
¼ tsp. (1.2 mL) malt powder or ½ tsp. (2.5 mL) granulated sugar
13⅓ oz. (380 g) unbleached hard white flour
6⅓ oz. (180 g) white dough starter at 55° to 61°F (13° to 16°C)
1¼ tsp. (6.2 mL) kosher or fine sea salt
6 oz. (170 g) coarsely grated cheddar + 1½ oz. (42 g) for topping
vegetable oil to grease a bowl

STARTER

In a small bowl, mix the yeast into the 1 Tbsp. + 1½ tsp. (22.5 mL) warm water. The yeast will take on a creamy consistency within a few minutes.

Pour the yeast into the bowl of a standing mixer with a dough hook. Add the cool water, flour, and salt.

Mix on slow (speed #2) for 1 minute. Scrape down the bowl with a plastic spatula as needed. Increase the speed to fast (speed #4) and mix for an additional 3 minutes.

continued ...

Lightly oil a bowl large enough to allow the starter to grow in size. Place the starter in the bowl and cover with plastic wrap.

Ferment the dough at room temperature, 70° to 74°F (21° to 24°C), in a draft-free area for 2 hours before transferring to the refrigerator: chill for 4 hours. Bring to 55° to 61°F (12° to 16°C) before proceeding with the recipe.

Alternatively, put the starter directly in the refrigerator for up to 12 to 13 hours, and then let rest, covered, on the counter at room temperature for about 1 hour or until it reaches a temperature of 55° to 61°F (12° to 16°C). Once it does, you can proceed with the recipe.

FINAL DOUGH

In the bowl of a standing mixer, combine the water, yeast, malt, and flour in the order listed. Stir with a spatula for 1 minute to bring the ingredients together. Using a dough hook, mix the dough for 2 minutes at fast (speed #4). Cover the bowl with a kitchen towel and let rest for 15 minutes.

Add the starter and salt to the dough and mix at slow (speed #2) for 2 minutes, followed by 3 minutes at fast (speed #4).

Add the cheese and mix at stir speed for 2 minutes. If the cheese is not fully incorporated into the dough, turn the dough onto a lightly floured counter. Flour your hands and gently knead in the cheese until it is just blended.

Lightly oil a bowl large enough to let the dough expand by about 50 percent.

Place the dough in the oiled bowl, turning it until it is covered in a thin layer of oil. This will prevent a crust from forming. Cover with plastic wrap and allow it to rise at room temperature in a draft-free area for 1 to 1½ hours or until it has increased in size by about 50 percent. The temperature of the dough should be approximately 75°F (24°C).

Weigh the dough and divide into 9 or 12 equal pieces. Nine pieces will yield sandwich-sized or large rolls while 12 will be good-sized dinner rolls. Roughly shape them into rounds by tucking the dough underneath itself. On a lightly floured surface, roll each piece of dough with the palm of your hand into a small ball. Lightly flour a baking tray and place the balls seam-side down in 3 rows of 3, or 4 rows of 4, just touching. Cover the dough with a kitchen towel or lightly oiled sheet of plastic wrap, and let sit at room temperature in a draft-free area for 45 minutes to 1 hour. If the dough starts to spread, flour your hands and gently reshape the dough back into rounds. The dough should have increased by about another 40 to 50 percent.

Meanwhile, preheat the oven to 400°F (200°C).

Spray the oven with water and close the door. Alternatively, place 6 to 8 ice cubes on the floor of the oven. Spray the rolls generously with water and immediately place the tray on the bottom rack of the oven. Bake for 10 minutes. Lower the temperature to 350°F (175°F). Sprinkle the extra cheese over the cluster and move the tray to the top rack. Bake for an additional 25 minutes.

Remove the tray from the oven and transfer the cluster to a cooling rack. Allow to rest for 1 hour before eating.

COOK'S TIP

TO MAKE BOULES (ROUNDS)

Divide the dough in 2 pieces of equal weight instead of 9 or 12 pieces for the rolls. Roughly shape them into rounds by tucking the dough underneath itself on a lightly floured surface. Place your hands on either side of the rough balls and gently rotate both your hands and the dough until the dough is smooth and rounded on top. Place, seam-side down, in a lightly oiled, shallow-lipped bowl slightly larger than the boule—some rimmed soup bowls work perfectly. Cover with a kitchen towel or with a piece of lightly oiled plastic wrap. Allow to rest in a draft–free area for 45 minutes to 1 hour. The dough should increase in size by about 40 to 50 percent. When it has, you can proceed with the recipe.

Flax Bread with Honey and Oats

MAKES 2 OVALS

If you're a novice bread baker, you'll find this recipe the easiest of the yeasted bread recipes in this book. We use organic ingredients when we make this bread at ACE. You can do the same, if so inclined. The benefit of the flax comes in its ground form. I like to make the starter the night before and, if I time it right, I can be eating the bread for lunch. You will soak the flax and rolled oats for an hour. After an initial mix, it will ferment for an hour or so. A bit of shaping on your part, followed by a resting period of another 1 to 1½ hours, and your dough is ready for the oven. You will be rewarded with two healthy and mouth-watering loaves (photo page 102) to share with family and friends.

OLD WHITE DOUGH (STARTER)
¾ tsp. (4 mL) traditional dry yeast
2½ tsp. (12.5 mL) lukewarm water at 75° to 90° F (24° to 32°C)
⅓ cup + 2 Tbsp. + ½ tsp. (112 mL) cool water at 65°F (18°C)
5.6 oz. (160 g) unbleached hard white flour
½ tsp. (2.5 mL) kosher or fine sea salt
vegetable oil to grease a bowl

FINAL DOUGH
1 oz. (30 g) golden flax seeds + extra for dusting the tops of the ovals
1 oz. (30 g) brown flax seeds
⅔ oz. (20 g) large rolled oats

⅓ cup (80 mL) lukewarm water at 75°F (24°C)
1 cup (240 mL) cool water at 65°F (18°C)
¾ tsp. (4 mL) traditional dry yeast
5½ oz. (155 g) unbleached hard white flour
5½ oz. (155 g) whole wheat hard flour
1 oz. (30 g) ground flax (see Cook's Tip)
½ tsp. (2.5 mL) malt powder or 1 Tbsp. (15 mL) white sugar
2½ tsp. (12.5 mL) wildflower or acacia honey
2 tsp. (10 mL) sunflower oil
9½ oz. (270 g) starter
1½ tsp. (7.5 mL) kosher or fine sea salt
sunflower oil to grease a bowl and brush the top of the finished dough

STARTER

In a small bowl mix the yeast into the 2½ tsp. (12.5 mL) warm water. The yeast will take on a creamy consistency within a few minutes.

Pour the yeast into the bowl of a standing mixer with a dough hook. Add the cool water, flour, and salt.

Mix on slow (speed #2) for 1 minute. Scrape down the bowl with a plastic spatula as needed. Increase the speed to fast (speed #4) and mix for an additional 3 minutes.

Lightly oil a bowl large enough to allow the starter to grow in size. Place the starter in the bowl and cover with plastic wrap.

Ferment the dough at room temperature, 70° to 74°F (21° to 24°C), in a draft-free area for 2 hours, before transferring to the refrigerator. Chill for 4 hours. Alternatively, immediately refrigerate the starter for 12 to 13 hours before continuing with the recipe.

Remove starter from refrigerator and let sit, covered, at room temperature for about 1 hour or until it reaches a temperature of 55° to 61°F (12° to 16°C). Once it does, you can proceed with the recipe.

FINAL DOUGH

In a small bowl, soak the golden and brown flax and the oats in the ⅓ cup (80 mL) lukewarm water for 1 hour or until all the liquid is absorbed.

Combine the cool water, yeast, white and whole wheat flours, ground flax, malt, honey, sunflower oil, and the soaked flax and oats in the bowl of a standing mixer. Stir with a spatula for 1 minute to mix the ingredients together. With the dough hook, mix the dough on stir speed for 3 minutes, and then on slow (speed #2) for another 4 minutes.

Cover the bowl with a kitchen towel to prevent the surface from drying and let it rest for 15 minutes.

Add the starter and salt to the dough and mix on slow (speed #2) for 2 minutes followed by fast (speed #4) for 1 more minute.

Lightly oil a bowl large enough to allow the dough to grow by one third.

To make it easier to remove the sticky dough from the mixing bowl, rub a thin layer of sunflower oil on the inside of your palms and fingers. Remove the dough from the standing mixer. If the dough is too sticky to shape, dust it with a bit of flour. Form into a ball and roll the dough in the oiled bowl so there is a thin layer of oil covering it. This will prevent a crust from forming on the surface. Cover with a towel or plastic wrap and leave the dough to ferment at room temperature in a draft-free area for 1 to 1½ hours. The dough will increase in size by about a third. Its temperature should be 73° to 75°F (23° to 24°C).

Divide the dough in half. Pat the two pieces into rough rectangles, about 8 × 5½ inches (20 × 13.7 cm). Use the palm of your hands to roll one long side of the dough toward the other like a long jelly roll. Pinch the seam together and lay the seam on the countertop. Gently shape the dough into 7- to 8-inch long (18- to 20-cm) ovals that are 3 inches (7.5 cm) wide. Carefully transfer to a baking tray. Cover with a towel or lightly oiled plastic wrap and let rest at room temperature in a draft-free area for an hour.

Meanwhile, preheat the oven to 375°F (190°C).

Brush the ovals with a thin layer of sunflower oil and dust with golden flax seeds.

Place the baking tray on the middle rack in the oven and spray the sides and bottom of the oven with water. Alternatively, place 6 to 8 ice cubes on the floor of the oven. Close the door immediately and bake for 40 minutes.

Remove the loaves from the oven and check if the bread is cooked by tapping the bottom with your fingertips. It should sound hollow. If not, return to the oven for several minutes more. Transfer to a cooling rack for at least an hour before cutting into it. Not all the flaxseeds will stay on the bread.

Store your bread in a paper or cloth bag. Do not refrigerate or use a plastic bag as a storing method. Refrigeration will draw the moisture out of the bread and a plastic bag will soften the crust.

COOK'S TIP

If you can't find ground flax, finely grind whole golden flax in a spice grinder.

Rosemary Olive Oil Grissini

MAKES 28 PIECES

If your experience with breadsticks has left you with the taste of sawdust in your mouth, you're in for a treat when you try these grissini (photo page 89). The addition of a pre-ferment (starter), olive oil, and sea salt in these rustic breadsticks makes for a deliciously crunchy treat.

If you make the starter the night before, you can be munching on grissini in about 2 hours, but your total working time is really about half an hour. You will have two periods of mixing interspersed with one short resting period, a fermentation time of about 1 hour, and a final 15-minute resting period.

Your biggest challenge, but also the most fun, is rolling the pieces of dough into about twenty-eight 14-inch (36-cm) cylinders. You can double the quantity by making fifty-six 7-inch (18-cm) grissini but, by doing so, you will lose the dramatic effect of the longer version.

STARTER

¼ tsp. (1.2 mL) traditional dry yeast

1 Tbsp. + 1½ tsp. (22.5 mL) lukewarm water at 75° to 90°F (24° to 32°C)

⅓ cup (80 mL) cool water at 65°F (18°C)

4½ oz. (128 g) unbleached hard white flour

½ tsp. (2.5 mL) kosher salt or fine sea salt

vegetable oil to grease a bowl

FINAL DOUGH

1 cup (240 mL) cool water at 65° to 68°F (18° to 20°C)

½ cup + 2 Tbsp. (150 mL) extra-virgin olive oil + oil to grease a bowl

½ tsp. (2.5 mL) traditional dry yeast

¼ tsp. (1.2 mL) malt powder or ½ tsp. (2.5 mL) granulated sugar

13⅓ oz. (380 g) unbleached white hard flour

6⅓ oz. (180 g) starter at 55° to 61°F (12° to 16°C)

1½ tsp. (7.5 mL) kosher or fine sea salt

2 generous tsp. (10 mL) minced fresh rosemary

coarsely ground black pepper

medium ground sea salt

1 egg white + 1½ tsp. (7.5 mL) water

STARTER

In a small bowl, mix the yeast into the lukewarm water. The yeast will take on a creamy consistency within a few minutes.

Pour the yeast into the bowl of a standing mixer with a dough hook and add the cool water, flour, and salt.

Mix on slow (speed #2) for 1 minute. Scrape down the bowl with a plastic spatula as needed. Increase the speed to fast (speed #4) and mix for an additional 3 minutes.

Lightly oil a bowl large enough to allow the starter to grow in size by one-quarter to one-third. Place the starter in the bowl and cover with plastic wrap.

Allow the dough to ferment at room temperature in a draft-free area for 2 hours, before transferring to the refrigerator for 4 hours. Alternatively, place the covered bowl directly in the refrigerator for up to 12 to 13 hours. Remove starter from refrigerator and let rest, covered, on the counter at room temperature for about 1 hour or until the starter reaches 55° to 61°F (12° to 16°C) before proceeding with the recipe.

Put the cool water, olive oil, yeast, malt powder, and flour into the bowl of a standing mixer and stir with a rubber spatula for 1 minute to thoroughly mix the ingredients. Add the dough hook to the mixer and follow with 2 minutes of mixing at fast (speed #4). Cover the bowl with a towel and let the dough rest for 15 minutes.

Lightly oil the inside of another bowl large enough to allow all the dough to expand by 30 to 50 percent.

Add the starter, kosher or fine sea salt, and rosemary to the dough and mix at slow (speed #2) for 2 minutes, followed by 4 minutes at fast (speed #4).

Remove the dough from the mixer and place in the oiled bowl. Roll the dough so that it is covered in a thin film of oil to prevent a crust from forming. Cover with plastic wrap or a towel and let it rise at room temperature, in a draft-free area, for 1¼ to 1½ hours.

Remove the dough from the bowl and place it on a lightly floured surface. Shape it into a rough circle about 10 inches (25 cm) in diameter. With a sharp knife, cut the dough in half and then in quarters. Roll each quarter into a cylinder and cut into 7 equal pieces.

Roll each piece into a 4-inch (10-cm) cylinder between the palms of your hands. Once rolled, place each cylinder on an unfloured work surface. (A floured surface will make it difficult to roll the dough.) Put the palms of your hands over the cylinders and begin to roll your hands in opposite directions, palms still in contact with the dough. This should be a fairly rapid movement and you will be stretching the dough as your hands separate. Repeat this action 7 or 8 times with each roll of dough until it is about 14 inches (36 cm) in length. Don't be concerned if they are not even. It will add a rustic charm to the finished grissini.

Place each grissini about ½ inch (1.2 cm) apart on a parchment-lined baking tray or cookie sheet.

Once all the dough is rolled out and placed on the trays, gently cover with a kitchen towel or oiled plastic wrap and let rest at room temperature for 15 minutes.

As the bread is resting, preheat the oven to 360°F (182°C).

Remove the towel. Brush the sticks very lightly with the egg white/water mixture. Sprinkle the tops generously with coarsely ground black pepper and medium coarse sea salt and immediately put the trays in the oven.

Check the grissini after 25 minutes. The top tray will be ready first. Test by piercing a stick with a skewer: it should feel consistently hard all the way through. Remove each grissini tray when ready, moving the trays up as you take one from the oven, and transfer the grissini to cooling racks. The egg wash may cause some of the grissini to stick to the baking tray. Remove them with a metal spatula.

You can enjoy the fruits of your labour immediately, but they will be even better the next day. Grissini will keep for 4 to 5 days at room temperature.

Pear, Hazelnut and Oatmeal Scones

Cheddar Chive Biscuits p. 30

Pear, Hazelnut and Oatmeal Scones

MAKES 8 LARGE TRIANGLE SCONES

I love the combination of dried pears—underused gems in my opinion—ginger, and hazelnuts. Substituting some of the flour with oatmeal adds a textural interest, and the sour cream counteracts the sweetness of the dried fruit, allowing the pears to shine through. Try the scones warm with a bit of unsalted butter or as an easy dessert paired with a fresh pear-lemon grass compote and a generous serving of whipped cream. The scones freeze well, so don't hesitate to make a double batch.

2 cups (475 mL) unbleached all-purpose flour
¼ cup (60 mL) granulated sugar
½ tsp. (2.5 mL) baking soda
1½ tsp. (7.5 mL) baking powder
1 tsp. (5 mL) kosher salt
1 cup (240 mL) rolled oats
¾ cup + 2 Tbsp. (210 mL) cold, unsalted butter, cut into ¼-inch (6-mm) cubes

⅓ cup + 1 Tbsp. (95 mL) 18% cream + 1 to 2 Tbsp. (15 to 30 mL) for brushing tops
½ cup (120 mL) sour cream
⅔ cup (160 mL) chopped dried pears
⅓ cup (80 mL) hazelnuts, chopped
1 tsp. (5 mL) grated fresh ginger
1 scant Tbsp. (15 mL) Demerara sugar

Preheat the oven to 375°F (190°C).

Sift the flour, sugar, baking soda, baking powder, and salt together into a bowl large enough to hold all the ingredients. Stir in the rolled oats until well mixed.

Add the butter and using your fingers, combine it with the dry ingredients until the mixture resembles a coarse meal.

In a separate bowl, whisk together the cream and sour cream until just blended. Add the liquids to the flour mixture along with the pears, hazelnuts, and ginger; stir until just combined, being careful not to overmix. Mix in 1 Tbsp. (15 mL) more cream, if needed, to bring the dough together.

Shape the dough into a ball and flatten into a 1¼-inch thick (3-cm) disk about 8 inches (20 cm) in diameter. Cut into 8 triangles. Brush lightly with cream and sprinkle with Demerara sugar.

Place on a lightly greased cookie sheet or parchment-lined sheet and bake on the middle rack of the oven for 15 minutes. Rotate the cookie sheet and bake 10 minutes more. Transfer the scones to a cooling rack for 10 to 15 minutes before serving.

COOK'S TIPS

1. Our daughter, Devin, makes these scones without the granulated sugar when she wants to serve them with cheese.

2. Dried apricots would make a good substitute if you can't find dried pears. You could also use dried apples with walnuts.

Pears have been cultivated for over 3000 years. If left on the tree to ripen fully, pears become mealy, which is why this fruit is picked when it is still green. The ripening process is completed as the pears are being transported, sold in grocery stores, and stored in your home.

Cheddar Chive Biscuits

MAKES 12 BISCUITS

Don't stint on the quality of cheddar you use in this recipe. And make sure it is aged and has a bit of a bite. I suggest you do a taste test to make sure you are happy with the flavour before you start baking. I like to pile scrambled eggs on top of these biscuits (photo page 28) for a quick and tasty breakfast or pair them with the Red Pepper and Corn Soup (see page 84) for an easy, late summer lunch.

2 ¾ cups (660 mL) unbleached all-purpose flour
1½ tsp. (7.5 mL) baking powder
¼ tsp. (1.2 mL) cayenne pepper
1½ tsp. (7.5 mL) kosher salt
¾ cup (180 mL) cold unsalted butter, cut into ¼-inch (6-mm) cubes

2 cups (475 mL) lightly packed, finely grated 2- to 3-year-old white cheddar + ¼ cup (60 mL) for topping
¼ cup (60 mL) minced fresh chives
1 cup + 2 Tbsp. (270 mL) 18% cream

Preheat the oven to 375°F (190°C).

Sift the flour, baking powder, cayenne pepper, and salt together in a bowl large enough to hold all the ingredients.

Using a pastry cutter, two knives, or your fingers, combine the butter with the dry ingredients until the mixture resembles a coarse meal.

Add 2 cups (475 mL) cheese and the chives to the flour mixture and mix in gently with a fork.

Add ½ cup (120 mL) of the cream and mix with your hands or a fork. Add another ½ cup (120 mL) of cream and continue mixing. Add up to 2 Tbsp. (30 mL) more cream if needed to keep the dough just together but not too sticky.

Shape the dough into a ball, and on a surface lightly dusted with flour, roll out into a ¾-inch (1.9-cm) thick round. Using a 2½-inch (6.2-cm) diameter round cookie cutter, cut out as many scones as possible and place on an ungreased cookie sheet. Gather the remaining dough together into a ball and repeat the rolling out and cutting process, always being careful to handle the dough as little as possible.

Bake for 15 minutes, rotate the cookie sheet, and sprinkle each biscuit with the remaining cheddar cheese. Bake for about 10 minutes more or until the tops are golden. Transfer the biscuits to a cooling rack for 10 to 15 minutes before serving.

COOK'S TIP

The dough can be made ahead of time and frozen—just defrost overnight in the refrigerator before cutting out the biscuits and baking. If you want to bake them while still cold, but not frozen, increase the oven temperature to 400°F (200°C).

Decadent Banana Date Bran Muffins

MAKES 6 LARGE MUFFINS OR 8 REGULAR MUFFINS

I would urge you to make a double batch of these delicious muffins, which freeze well. When you need a treat in the morning, at the start of a potentially difficult day, they will do the trick. As the title indicates, these muffins are quite rich, so I sometimes serve them as a casual dessert with a simple fruit salad and a dollop of sweetened crème fraîche.

1 cup (240 mL) red wheat bran or wheat bran
¼ cup (60 mL) whole milk
¾ cup (180 mL) buttermilk
½ cup (120 mL) lightly packed brown sugar
¾ cup + 2 Tbsp. (210 mL) all-purpose flour
1 tsp. (5 mL) baking soda
1½ tsp. (7.5 mL) kosher salt

¼ tsp. (1.2 mL) ground nutmeg
1 medium to large banana
1 large egg
⅓ cup (80 mL) melted unsalted butter
generous ½ cup (120 mL) pitted chopped
   dates, about 10 dates

Preheat the oven to 350°F (190°C).

Mix the bran, milk, and ¼ cup (60 mL) of the buttermilk in a small bowl and set aside to soak for 30 minutes.

In a medium to large bowl, whisk together the brown sugar, flour, baking soda, salt, and nutmeg to aerate slightly and to break up any large clumps of sugar.

In a smaller mixing bowl, mash the banana with a fork until smooth. Stir in the egg, butter, dates, the remaining ½ cup (120 mL) buttermilk, and the soaked bran.

Add the banana mixture to the dry ingredients and stir gently until just combined.

Pour the batter into a large cupped greased muffin pan and bake for approximately 20 to 25 minutes, rotating the pan 10 minutes into the baking time.

The muffins are done when a skewer, inserted into the middle of one, comes out glistening but not covered in dough. When the muffins are cool enough to handle, remove from the pan and cool on a wire rack for another 15 to 20 minutes before serving.

Angel Muffins

These muffins have been a long-time favourite at the ACE Fresh Bread Store and Café. When testing this recipe, we found three things that make a great difference to their ultimate texture. First, the type of flour. All-purpose simply won't do the trick. Second, the stiffness of the egg whites. The whites will become slightly liquid again when you add the sugar and flour. If the whites are too liquid at this point, the muffins will be tough. Finally, the temperature of the oven. Halfway through the baking time the muffins should just be turning golden brown on their points. If they are too dark or too pale, adjust your oven temperature accordingly.

1¼ cups (300 mL) cake and pastry flour
1 tsp. (5 mL) kosher salt
3½ oz. (100 g) dried apricots, about 11
9 extra-large egg whites, at room temperature

2 Tbsp. (30 mL) water
2½ tsp. (12.5 mL) cream of tartar
1 tsp. (5 mL) pure vanilla extract
¾ cup + 2 Tbsp. (210 mL) fine white sugar

Preheat the oven to 325°F (165°C).

Sift the flour and stir in the salt.

Finely chop the apricots, dusting with a touch of the flour mixture as you go to keep them from sticking together and forming large clumps, or use a pair of clean, sharp scissors to cut the fruit into small pieces.

Whip the egg whites and water together in a standing mixer on high speed until just foamy. Add the cream of tartar and continue whipping at high speed until the egg whites form very stiff peaks.

Change the mixing speed to medium and add the vanilla. Gradually add all the sugar while still whipping.

Fold in the sifted flour in 4 separate additions.

Gently fold in the apricots.

Spoon the batter into a paper cup-lined large muffin pan, mounding the batter about ½ to ¾ inches (1.2 to 1.9 cm) over the top of each muffin cup. The top should be light and fluffy and irregular in appearance. Bake for 12 to 13 minutes. Rotate the muffin tray and bake 12 minutes more.

Remove the muffins from the pan and transfer to a rack until cool.

COOK'S TIP

If you don't have fine or superfine white sugar, grind some regular granulated sugar in the food processor for a minute or so.

Orange Almond Tea Loaf

MAKES 1 LOAF

When you've had enough of lemon loaf, this is a light and fresh alternative. I've used all-purpose flour but if you like a lighter, softer crumb, substitute cake flour in equal amounts. This tea loaf will keep fresh, if wrapped well, on your counter for 2 to 3 days. Lightly toast any leftovers and spread with unsalted butter for a treat at breakfast.

⅓ cup (80 mL) almond slivers, not flakes
½ cup (120 mL) softened unsalted butter, plus butter to grease the loaf pan
¾ cup + 1 Tbsp. (195 mL) granulated sugar
2 large eggs, at room temperature
1 tsp. (5 mL) vanilla extract
1½ cups (360 mL) all-purpose flour

1½ tsp. (7.5 mL) baking soda
¾ tsp. (4 mL) kosher salt
½ cup (120 mL) homogenized milk, at room temperature
3 Tbsp. (45 mL) finely grated organic orange zest (2 to 3 medium to large oranges)

Heat the oven to 350°F (175°C).

Toast the almonds until golden brown, about 3 minutes. Cool, roughly chop, and reserve.

Butter and flour a 4½- × 8-inch (11.2- × 20-cm) good quality loaf pan.

Cream the butter and sugar together with an electric mixer in a bowl large enough to hold all the ingredients. In a small bowl, whisk together the eggs and vanilla before mixing them into the butter-and-sugar mixture.

Sift together the flour, baking soda, and salt before adding to the butter and sugar mixture; mix well until the batter is smooth. Gently mix in the milk then fold in the orange zest and the almonds.

Pour the batter into the pan and bake for about 60 to 70 minutes, or until a cake tester comes out clean.

Rest the pan on a cooling rack for 10 minutes before turning out the cake to finish cooling.

Serve at room temperature.

Wrapped in plastic wrap, the loaf will keep at room temperature for 2 to 3 days.

COOK'S TIPS

1. To make fast and easy work of zesting any citrus fruit, use a Microplane grater. They are available in most kitchenware stores.

2. To quickly butter a baking pan, melt a small amount of unsalted butter in a saucepan and brush it on the inside surfaces of the pan with a pastry brush.

Baguette Flatbread

MAKES 12 TO 18 PIECES

Sometimes I purposely let a baguette go stale so I can make this delicious "flatbread." It looks especially nice mixed with other bread and sticking up in a bread basket (photo page 74).

1 day-old baguette
3 to 6 Tbsp. (45 to 90 mL) olive oil or melted
  unsalted butter
2 tsp. (10 mL) kosher or fine sea salt, or to
  taste
4 Tbsp. (60 mL) freshly grated Parmigiano
  Reggiano or old white cheddar (optional)

Preheat the oven to 400°F (200°C).

Cut the baguette in half or in thirds. Slice off both sides of the crust, leaving only the top and bottom crust. Carefully slice ⅛- to ¼-inch thick (3- to 6-mm) slices, lengthwise through the top and down the side of the baguette.

Brush both sides of the slices with either olive oil or butter and place on a baking sheet. Sprinkle one side with either salt or cheese.

Bake just below the broiling position (second rack) of the oven for about 10 to 15 minutes or until the top is golden brown. They will brown more quickly if you use butter. The bottoms should have browned also. If not, turn and bake for another minute or two.

Jim's Sage, Pecan and Dried Fruit Stuffing

MAKES ENOUGH FOR ONE (8 TO 12 LB./3.9 TO 5.4 KG) TURKEY

Jim Rossler, a former chef now working in sales at ACE Bakery, came up with this recipe to promote the sage bread that we sell from late Fall through Christmas. I've adapted the ingredients to include fresh sage and white bread in case you aren't in an area where ACE breads are sold. If you are, use half the fresh sage called for in the recipe. You'll be happy if you make a few more candied pecans as they are terrific served with drinks.

1 large loaf white bread, sliced with crusts on
1 cup (240 mL) fresh or frozen cranberries
½ cup (120 mL) unsweetened apple juice
1¼ cup (300 mL) finely diced Spanish onion
1 cup (240 mL) diced dried figs
½ cup (120 mL) coarsely chopped Sugared
  Pecans (see opposite page)

4 Tbsp. (60 mL) finely chopped fresh sage
⅓ cup (75 mL) melted unsalted butter
½ cup (120 mL) turkey or chicken stock
2 tsp. (10 mL) kosher salt
8 grinds freshly ground black pepper

Preheat the oven to 375°F (190°C).

Dice the bread into ½-inch (1.2-cm) square chunks and spread on a baking sheet. Toast in the oven until crisp but not browned, about 5 to 8 minutes. Transfer to a bowl large enough to hold all the ingredients.

Put the cranberries and ¼ cup (60 mL) apple juice into a saucepan and bring to a boil. Reduce heat to low and simmer 1 minute. Drain the cranberries, discarding the cooked apple juice, and add to the bread, along with the onion, figs, sugared pecans, and sage.

Whisk together the remaining ¼ cup (60 mL) apple juice, butter, and stock. Gently toss into the bread. Season with salt and pepper and add a little more stock if necessary.

Stuff the turkey just before roasting or bake, covered, in a low-sided casserole dish at 375°F (190°C) for 50 minutes.

"No more turkey, but I'll take more of the bread it ate."

—Hank Ketcham

Sugared Pecans

MAKES 1 CUP (240 ML)

1 egg white
2 Tbsp. (30 mL) Demerara sugar
2 tsp. (10 mL) coarse sea salt
1 cup (240 mL) shelled pecan halves

Preheat the oven to 325°F (165°C).

In a small bowl, lightly whisk the egg white with a fork. Stir in the sugar and salt, and continue whisking until well mixed. Add the pecans and toss until well coated. Remove the nuts with a slotted spoon, shaking 2 or 3 times, and place in a sieve to drain for half an hour, making sure they are just very lightly coated with the egg white mixture. If the nuts still have a thick coating of egg white, toss them again with a slotted spoon.

Place the pecans, in one layer, on a parchment-lined baking tray and roast for 15 minutes, until the coating has hardened.

Remove from the oven and allow to cool.

Pecans, indigenous to North America, grow in clusters on the tree. They are ready to be harvested when the nut starts to crack. Because they have a more than 70% fat content, they will turn rancid if left unrefrigerated for any period of time.

Breakfast

Jamaican Banana Fritters   40

Stilton and Leek Flans   42

Oven-Baked Mango Pancake   43

Cheddar and Bacon Stuffed French Toast with Maple-Glazed Pears   45

Gratinéed Asparagus, Tomato and Chèvre Frittata   47

Corn, Chili and Cheese Strata with Avocado Salsa   49

Strawberry Mint Jam   51

Banana Crush   52

Kiwi Lassi   54

Pineapple Papaya Frosty   55

Spiced Hot Chocolate   56

"Life, within doors, has fewer pleasanter prospects than a neatly arranged and well-provisioned breakfast table."
—Nathaniel Hawthorne

Jamaican Banana Fritters

MAKES ABOUT 20 FRITTERS

Many years ago, when our children were toddlers, we rented a house named Almond Tree, in Jamaica. Ms. Lynn, the cook, would make mouth-watering fritters for breakfast. Our kids couldn't wait to get to the table. On the last day of our trip she slipped the recipe into my luggage. Even today, when I make them, Devin and Luke say a quiet thank you to Ms. Lynn.

2 Tbsp. (30 mL) granulated sugar
¼ tsp. (1.2 mL) baking powder
1 cup (240 mL) all-purpose flour
¼ cup (60 mL) raisins or currants
pinch ground nutmeg
pinch ground cinnamon
pinch kosher salt

4 small ripe bananas
1 egg, lightly whisked
½ tsp. (2.5 mL) vanilla extract
2 to 4 Tbsp. (30 to 60 mL) vegetable oil
ground nutmeg and white sugar for dusting
juice of 1 lime or 2 limes cut in quarters

Toss the sugar, baking powder, flour, raisins, nutmeg, cinnamon, and salt together in a small bowl.

In another bowl large enough to hold all the ingredients, mash the bananas. Stir in the egg, vanilla, and the sugar mixture. Mix until well blended.

Heat 2 Tbsp. (30 mL) of oil in a frying pan over medium heat. (A cube of bread dropped in the oil should turn golden brown in about 1 minute.) Drop the batter in by heaping tablespoonfuls and fry until golden brown on both sides. Heat more oil in the skillet as needed as you will be frying the batter in batches. Drain on a paper towel and keep warm. The fritters can be held in a 325°F (165°C) oven for 30 minutes.

Sprinkle with nutmeg and sugar and serve with a drizzle of lime juice or lime quarters.

COOK'S TIP
For a darker golden, richer fritter, substitute butter for half the oil.

Stilton and Leek Flans

MAKES 6 (1-CUP/240-ML) FLANS

I've served these flans for brunch, as a first course before the Rosemary Skewered Grilled Shrimp on Summer Vegetables (see page 155), as a side dish with roasted chicken and even as a substitute for a cheese course. If you wish to serve them for brunch, pork sausages, with a big green salad and plenty of multigrain or whole wheat toast, would be the perfect complement.

1 heaping cup (240 mL) loosely packed, very thinly sliced leeks (white and light green parts)
1 Tbsp. (15 mL) corn oil
4 large eggs
1 cup (240 mL) 18% cream
½ cup (120 mL) homogenized milk

¼ tsp. (1.2 mL) ground nutmeg
½ tsp. (2.5 mL) kosher salt
⅛ tsp. (0.5 mL) freshly ground black pepper
½ cup (120 mL) crumbled Stilton cheese
1 Tbsp. (15 mL) unsalted butter
⅔ cup (160 mL) fresh breadcrumbs

Preheat the oven to 325°F (165°C).

Place the sliced leeks in a small bowl and fill with cold water. Let sit for 10 minutes or until the dirt from the leeks has settled to the bottom of the bowl. Drain and pat dry.

Pour the oil into a small frying pan and sauté the leeks over medium heat until they have softened, but not changed colour.

In a mixing bowl, whisk the eggs together with the cream and milk. Add the nutmeg, salt, and pepper and continue whisking for a few seconds more.

Lightly grease six 1-cup (240-mL) ramekins. Divide the Stilton and the leeks evenly among the ramekins, then pour in the egg mixture. Place the ramekins in a *bain marie* (see below) and transfer to the oven. Bake for about 30 minutes or until the custard is set. If the flans start to brown on top, cover with tin foil.

While the flans are baking, melt the butter in a small frying pan over medium-low heat and sauté the breadcrumbs until golden.

Remove the flans from the oven when they are set and sprinkle with breadcrumbs.

A bain marie is the French term for a water bath. Place the flans in a high-sided oven pan in the oven and use a kettle or indoor watering can to pour warm water a third of the way up the sides of the dishes. This will allow the flans to gently cook and not "scramble" the eggs.

Oven-Baked Mango Pancake

SERVES 4 TO 6

This is a great recipe to make if you are having guests for breakfast or brunch and don't want to be left alone in the kitchen. I make it when I have a craving for pancakes but don't want to stand over a hot stove, spatula in hand. Simply peel some fruit, take five minutes to mix the dough, another thirty minutes in the oven, and an elegant dish is on the table. Drizzle with a touch of warm maple syrup or honey and serve with oven-baked sausages.

1 small mango, about 1 generous cup (240 mL) diced flesh
2 large eggs, at room temperature
3 Tbsp. (45 mL) granulated sugar + 1 Tbsp. (15 mL) for dusting
⅔ cup (160 mL) all-purpose flour

pinch kosher salt
1 cup (240 mL) whole milk, at room temperature
1 Tbsp. (15 mL) softened unsalted butter
maple syrup or honey (optional)

Preheat the oven to 425°F (220°C). As the oven is heating, put an 8- to 10-inch (20- to 25-cm) cast iron pan in the oven on the lowest rack to heat.

Peel and pit the mango and cut into ½-inch (1.2-cm) dice.

In a bowl, whisk together the eggs and 3 Tbsp. (45 mL) sugar. Sift the flour into the egg mixture in two batches and mix in along with the salt. Slowly whisk in the milk until a batter forms. Don't be concerned if the batter is not perfectly smooth. Mix in the mango.

Carefully remove the hot cast iron pan from the oven. Add the butter and rotate and tilt the pan to form an even coating of melted butter on the bottom and sides of the pan. Once the butter has melted, pour the pancake batter into the pan, making sure the mango is evenly distributed.

Bake for 30 minutes or until puffed and dark golden. Remove from the oven, and turn on the broiler. Sprinkle the top of the pancake with the remaining 1 Tbsp. (15 mL) sugar. Return the pan to the top rack of the oven; broil until the sugar has melted, about 1 minute.

Serve immediately with a drizzle of warm maple syrup or honey.

COOK'S TIP

Substitute bananas, peaches or sautéed apples or pears for the mangoes.

Cheddar and Bacon Stuffed French Toast with Maple-Glazed Pears

SERVES 2

This is the ultimate make-ahead dish for a lazy weekend meal. You can prep the French toast up until the moment it gets popped in the oven and also sauté the pears. When ready to serve, and if stored in the refrigerator, bring the toast and the pears to room temperature, bake the toast, gently heat up the fruit, and you're ready to sit down. A glass of champagne and orange juice would be just the thing to propose a toast to the chef.

two 1½-inch (3.8-cm) slices dense white or
    Calabrese bread
2 thin slices Canadian bacon (also called back
    or peameal bacon)
4 to 8 thin slices of 2- to 3-year-old white
    cheddar or Gruyère

2 large eggs
1 cup (240 mL) whole milk
⅛ tsp. (0.5 mL) minced fresh thyme
pinch kosher salt
1 Tbsp. (15 mL) unsalted butter
MAPLE-GLAZED PEARS (SEE PAGE 46)

Preheat the oven to 400°F (200°C).

Starting at the bottom part of the 2 slices of bread, cut a horizontal pocket large enough and deep enough to hold the bacon and cheese. Don't cut through the top or sides of the bread.

Fry the bacon over medium heat until golden, 1 to 1½ minutes per side. Pat with paper towels and reserve.

Stuff each piece of bread with a slice or two of cheese, followed by a piece of bacon and another layer of cheese.

Whisk the eggs, milk, thyme, and salt together in a shallow bowl large enough to hold both pieces of bread.

Soak the stuffed bread in the egg mixture for 1 minute. Turn over and soak for another minute. Discard any leftover liquid.

Melt the butter in a frying pan large enough to hold both sandwiches. Fry the bread on both sides until golden, about 1 to 1½ minutes per side.

Transfer the French toast to an ovenproof dish and bake for 10 minutes. Remove stuffed toast slices from dish to a cutting board and slice each in half diagonally. Place 2 halves on each of two plates, garnish with pears, and drizzle with maple glaze.

COOK'S TIP

For a change of pace, you may like to make "French toast coins." Cut white or Calabrese baguette into ½- to ¾-inch (1.2- to 1.9-cm) slices. Layer with cheese, bacon, and more cheese. Dip in the egg mixture and follow the cooking instructions in the main recipe. Bake for 5 minutes in the oven instead of 10.

Maple-Glazed Pears

MAKES ½ – ¾ CUP (120–180 mL)

1 Tbsp. (15 mL) unsalted butter
1 Bosc or other cooking pear, peeled, cored
  and sliced lengthwise ⅛-inch (3-mm) thick
⅛ tsp. (0.5 mL) minced fresh thyme
2 Tbsp. (30 mL) maple syrup

Melt butter over medium-low heat in a nonstick frying pan. Add the pears and thyme and sauté for 3 to 4 minutes, making sure the pears don't break up or turn brown. Pour in the maple syrup and quickly toss pears to coat all sides. Simmer for about 30 seconds to 1 minute or until the syrup and the liquid from the pears have melded into a glaze. Remove from heat and serve immediately over the plated French toast halves.

Cheddar, originally produced in England, was never legally protected or defined. Consequently, many cheeses today incorrectly bear the name. True cheddar has a slightly dry texture, with a range of nutty, fruity, and sharp flavours.

Gratinéed Asparagus, Tomato and Chèvre Frittata

SERVES 6 TO 8, DEPENDING ON APPETITE

I find eggs have a natural affinity with almost any vegetable or cheese, but the combination of asparagus, tomatoes, and chèvre mixed with green onion and tarragon is truly special. A gratinée of breadcrumbs and Parmigiano Reggiano seems to be a fitting finish. I like to use a nonstick pan so I can easily slide the frittata onto a pretty serving plate. The Boston lettuce salad (see page 100), minus the Gruyère, works well as an accompaniment when serving this for brunch.

8 asparagus stalks
½ cup (120 mL) fresh breadcrumbs
2 Tbsp. + 2 tsp. (40 mL) unsalted butter
½ cup (120 mL) grated Parmigiano Reggiano
3 green onions, white and light green part, thinly sliced
9 large eggs

¾ tsp. (4 mL) kosher salt
8 cherry tomatoes, seeded and cut in strips
3 oz. (85 g) creamy mild chèvre, crumbled, about ⅓ cup (80 mL)
1 tsp. (5 mL) minced fresh tarragon
¼ tsp. (1.2 mL) coarsely ground black pepper

Clean and boil the asparagus until cooked but still a bit crisp. Plunge into cold water, to preserve the colour, and drain. Cut into 1-inch (2.5-cm) pieces but reserve three tips 3-inches (7.5-cm) long. Set the 3 tips aside.

In a small frying pan, sauté the breadcrumbs in 1 Tbsp. (15 mL) melted butter until toasted and golden. Cool, and mix with the Parmigiano Reggiano. In the same frying pan, lightly sauté the green onions in 2 tsp. (10 mL) melted butter.

Preheat the broiler.

Whisk the eggs with the salt in a small bowl. Melt the remaining 1 Tbsp. (15 mL) butter over medium heat in a 9- to 10-inch (23- to 25-cm) sauté or frying pan until it just bubbles. Make sure to coat the sides of the pan with butter as well as the bottom—a nonstick pan is preferable.

Turn the heat to medium-low, pour the eggs into the pan, and cook for 1 minute. Evenly distribute the tomatoes, the 1-inch (2.5-cm) pieces of asparagus, the chèvre, onions, and tarragon over the eggs and grind on the pepper. Cover the pan with a lid and continue cooking for about 8 to 10 minutes or until the frittata has puffed slightly around the edges and there is just a glistening of liquid egg still visible in the middle.

Remove the frittata from the heat and sprinkle with the breadcrumbs. Place under the broiler for no more than 2 minutes.

Decorate the middle of the frittata with the reserved 3-inch pieces of asparagus. Serve immediately from the pan or, if you are using a nonstick pan, slide the frittata onto a warm serving dish. Serve with warm slices of baguette or whole grain bread.

COOK'S TIP

To make fresh breadcrumbs, process 2 or 3 slices of fresh bread (no more than one day old) in the food processor until you have light fluffy crumbs.

Corn, Chili and Cheese Strata with Avocado Salsa

SERVES 6

I have assembled this strata the afternoon before I wanted to serve it, chilled it in the refrigerator overnight, brought it to room temperature, and baked it while having drinks with my guests. But it's just as good prepared the same day you will be eating it, as long as the strata soaks in the egg mixture for at least 30 minutes. The Avocado Salsa can be made an hour or so before you sit down. This is a delicately spiced version so feel free to add more jalapeño pepper and chili powder if you want a bigger kick.

10 to 12 slices white bread
1½ Tbsp. (22.5 mL) corn oil
1½ cups (360 mL) lightly packed, finely sliced cooking onion
¾ cup (180 mL) grated 3-year-old white cheddar
¾ cup (180 mL) grated Monterey Jack cheese
1 cup (240 mL) uncooked fresh corn (2 to 3 ears) or thawed frozen corn
1½ tsp. (7.5 mL) minced fresh jalapeño pepper, or more, to taste

4 large eggs
1½ cups (360 mL) homogenized milk
1¼ cups (300 mL) 18% cream
1 tsp. (5 mL) kosher salt
⅛ tsp. (1 mL) freshly ground black pepper
1 heaping tsp. (5 mL) chipotle chili powder
sour cream (optional)
AVOCADO SALSA (SEE PAGE 50)

Cut the slices of bread in half horizontally.

Pour the oil into a frying pan on medium heat and immediately add the onions. Sauté until soft, approximately 3 to 5 minutes, but not brown. Set aside.

Mix the two cheeses together, reserving ½ cup (120 mL) for the top of the strata.

Evenly place bread slice halves in a low casserole dish with a 7- to 8-cup (1.7- to 8-L) capacity, making sure the bottom of the dish is completely covered.

Sprinkle half the onion, then half the corn over the bread. Follow with half the minced jalapeño pepper and half the cheese. Top with another layer of bread and follow with the rest of the onions, corn, jalapeño pepper, and cheese. Cut the remainder of the bread into 1-inch (2.5-cm) cubes and sprinkle over the top.

In a medium bowl, whisk together the eggs, milk, cream, salt, pepper, and chili powder until well combined.

Pour the egg mixture over the strata, making sure to thoroughly soak the top layer of bread. Cover tightly with plastic wrap and let sit for at least 30 minutes.

Preheat the oven to 375°F (190°C).

Remove the wrap and bake for about 1 hour or until the custard is just set. The strata will have a puffy, soft look. Sprinkle the remaining cheese over the strata and bake another 5 to 10 minutes, until the top is golden. (You may want to quickly finish it off under the broiler for 1 to 2 minutes.)

Let the strata rest for 10 to 20 minutes before serving with sour cream and Avocado Salsa.

Avocado Salsa

1 firm but ripe medium to large avocado
3 Tbsp. (45 mL) minced red onion
⅓ cup (80 mL) seeded and minced tomato
½ tsp. (2.5 mL) minced jalapeño pepper, or
    more to taste
3 Tbsp. (45 mL) freshly squeezed lime juice
3 Tbsp. (45 mL) chopped fresh coriander
    (optional)

Peel the avocado and cut into cubes no larger than ½ inch (1.2 cm). In a medium bowl, gently toss the avocado with the remaining ingredients, making sure not to mash the avocado pieces.

COOK'S TIP FOR THE STRATA (SEE PAGE 49)

Putting the oil and onions into the pan at the same time will ensure that your onions will turn pale golden and won't burn as quickly.

Chipotle chili powder is made by drying and then smoking jalapeño peppers. You will find it in gourmet and Latin American grocery stores.

Strawberry Mint Jam

My husband, Martin, is the jam maker in the family. When the children were young it was a summer ritual. Now that they are older our jam supply has been dwindling. But occasionally Martin will spend a rainy summer afternoon over the stove making a batch. He follows the basic Larousse method—one that produces a thick, luscious confection very unlike what is available at most supermarkets. You will need 5 or 6 sterilized ½ cup (120 mL) Mason jars and a candy thermometer for this recipe (photo page 16).

1 cup (240 mL) water
1⅓ lbs. (600 g) granulated sugar
2 lbs. (900 g) strawberries, fresh or
   unsweetened frozen
1 4-inch (10-cm) sprig fresh mint

Bring the water to a boil in a medium to large saucepan over high heat. Add the sugar and stir until well mixed but not dissolved. Lower the heat to medium and add the fruit, stirring continuously for about 10 minutes or until the sugar has dissolved completely in the juices released by the strawberries. Strain the strawberries from the liquid with a slotted spoon and set aside.

Return the sugar and juice mixture to a boil and continue stirring. Once the mixture has begun to thicken, check the temperature with a candy thermometer. Keep stirring until it has reached 350°F (175°C), or the "soft ball" stage. This may take up to 30 minutes.

Add the reserved strawberries and the mint sprig and stir continuously for 5 to 10 minutes. Remove the mint sprig and discard. Ladle jam into hot, sterilized small preserving jars, leaving ½-inch (1.2-cm) headspace. Top with disk and loosely apply screwband. Process filled jars in a covered pan filled with water that reaches one-third of the way up the sides of the jars. Bring to a soft boil and cook for 15 minutes. Remove jars and, without tightening screwbands, place them upright on a rack to cool. After the jars have cooled, check for a seal. If the disk has snapped down (is curving downward), a seal has occurred. Tighten the lids. If a jar has not sealed, store it in the refrigerator. Label and store in a cool, dark and dry place.

COOK'S TIP

Occasionally Martin will freeze summer strawberries and make his jam later in the year. If you are using store-bought frozen berries, buy ones with no sugar added.

Sterilize your jars, tops, and screwbands by running them through a dishwashing cycle or by submerging them in a pot of boiling water for 10 minutes.

Banana Crush

SERVES 2

This is almost a meal in a glass. I occasionally make it for myself when I'm too rushed to sit down for breakfast. It's also refreshingly delicious mixed with a shot of dark rum on a hot summer afternoon.

1 medium banana
2 cups (480 mL) whole milk
1 cup (240 mL) ice cubes
ground nutmeg

Place the banana, milk, and ice in a blender and blend until smooth. Pour into 2 glasses and dust with nutmeg.

Bananas, which contain nearly 20% sugar, are the seedless berries of a tree-sized herb. The word "banana" comes from the Arabic word banan, which means finger. A stem of bananas can contain as many as 200 fruit and weigh over 80 pounds (37 kg).

Banana Crush

Pineapple Papaya
Frosty p. 55

Kiwi Lassi p. 54

Kiwi Lassi

SERVES 2

Lassi, a very popular drink in India, is sometimes half milk and half yogurt. A version of this recipe is served at breakfast at the Imperial Hotel in New Delhi. You can substitute mango, papaya, peaches, or even berries, for the kiwi. If you do use berries, press them through a strainer before blending with the rest of the ingredients (photo page 53).

    2 kiwis, peeled and cut in 1-inch (2.5-cm)
       chunks
    ⅔ (160 mL) cup low-fat yogurt
    ½ cup (120 mL) ice cubes
    2 Tbsp. (30 mL) granulated sugar

Place all the kiwi, yogurt, ice, and 1 Tbsp. (15 mL) sugar in a blender; blend until smooth. Add more sugar if necessary. Serve immediately. The kiwi will take on a bitter flavour about 30 minutes after blending.

A tart green berry from a Chinese vine, the kiwi was made popular by New Zealand growers. Slow to ripen during its long months of storage, the kiwi's starches are converted to sugar. It should be kept at room temperature for up to two weeks to fully ripen.

Pineapple Papaya Frosty

MAKES ABOUT 4 CUPS (950 ML)

Many years ago, on Tamarindo Beach in Costa Rica, a Swiss man had a stand that sold fabulous fruit drinks. We would stop by every afternoon on our way back from the beach and order a different combination each day. Our son Luke, though, fell in love with Pineapple Papaya Frosty (photo page 53). It became his daily ritual. Although our Swiss friend didn't serve alcohol in his frosty, we find adding a shot of tequila doesn't hurt.

2 cups (475 mL) peeled and chopped fresh
    pineapple (about half a pineapple)
1 small papaya, peeled, seeded and chopped,
    about 1½ cups (360 mL)
2 cups (475 mL) ice
½ cup (120 mL) pulp-free orange juice
sparkling water, champagne, or tequila
    (optional)
fresh mint sprigs for garnish

Place the pineapple, papaya, ice, and orange juice in a blender and blend until smooth. Wait a few minutes to serve so the ice can melt a bit and the fruit flavours come through. Stir in sparkling water, champagne, or tequila if you want to thin or flavour the drink. Pour into glasses and top with a sprig of mint.

Once a pineapple is harvested, it won't get any sweeter. It will, however, become softer and juicier if left at room temperature for a couple of days before being served.

Spiced Hot Chocolate

SERVES 2

This decadently rich drink could substitute for dessert if you had a mind to. The chili, vanilla, and cinnamon are a Mexican influence. The orange rounds out all the flavours. Use chocolate with 60 percent cocoa content.

2 oz. (57 g) semi-sweet chocolate
1½ cups (360 mL) 2% or homogenized milk
½- × 2½-inch (1.2- × 6.2-cm) strip orange
   rind
3 to 4 drops pure vanilla extract
1½ tsp. (7.5 mL) granulated sugar, or more,
   to taste
pinch ground chipotle pepper
⅛ tsp. (0.5 mL) ground cinnamon
2 Tbsp. (30 mL) dark rum (optional)
4 Tbsp. (60 mL) whipped cream (optional)

Chop or roughly grate the chocolate. Pour the milk into a small saucepan over medium heat and add the chocolate and orange rind. Stir occasionally until the chocolate is completely melted. Then mix in vanilla, sugar, chipotle pepper, and cinnamon. Add more sugar or spices if desired. Stir and remove from heat; discard the rind.

If using, add 1 Tbsp. (15 mL) of dark rum to each of two mugs. Pour in the hot chocolate and stir. Top each drink with a generous dollop of whipped cream.

"All I need is love, but a little chocolate now and then doesn't hurt."
—Lucy (in Peanuts by Charles M. Schulz)

When Spanish conqueror Hernando Cortez first discovered the vanilla bean in Mexico, he was interested in harnessing its powerful aroma for perfumes. However, when he observed the Aztec emperor, Montezuma, drinking vanilla-scented chocolate, he decided to bring the mixture back to Europe. This luxurious beverage became so popular that for 80 years the vanilla bean was used exclusively for this drink.

To Start

"Small cheer and great welcome make a merry feast."

—William Shakespeare

Lacy Parmigiano Crisps – Two Ways

Lovely to look at, simple to make and yummy to eat, serve these pretty crisps with drinks before dinner or as a "hat" to a salad. Your friends will think you have spent hours in the kitchen. Only you and I will know the truth.

2 cups finely grated Parmigiano Reggiano
4 Tbsp. (60 mL) finely chopped walnuts
OR
2 Tbsp. (30 mL) minced chives and
    ½ tsp. (2.5 mL) coarsely ground black pepper

Preheat the oven to 375°F (190°C).

Line 2 baking trays with parchment paper.

In a medium bowl, toss the cheese with the walnuts or the chives and black pepper.

Place the cheese mixture on the baking trays in 2-Tbsp. (30-mL) mounds, about 3 inches (7.5 cm) apart, until all the cheese mixture is gone.

Bake until the cheese is melted and bubbling and the crisps are flat and golden, about 3 to 5 minutes.

Remove from the oven and allow to sit for 1 to 2 minutes before carefully separating the crisps from the parchment paper.

These crisps are best eaten almost immediately but will keep in an airtight container for 24 hours.

COOK'S TIP

Wrap your Parmigiano Reggiano in wax or parchment paper, then in plastic wrap and store in the refrigerator. Change the wrapping every four or five days to allow the cheese to breath. Wrapped and stored this way the cheese will keep for up to 1 month.

Lemon Pepper Cashews p. 62

Lemon Pepper Cashews

I have often bought cashews tossed with cayenne pepper and salt in Indian grocery shops and restaurants. When I noticed a new Indian vegetarian restaurant in my neighbourhood I went in to buy my usual fix. They were selling see-through "cones" of both red and black pepper cashews. When I asked the owner about the black pepper-coated cashews (photo page 61), she told me she used lemon juice, salt, and black pepper to give the nuts a distinctive taste. This is my version of her spicy, addictive cashews.

1½ cups (360 mL) unsalted roasted cashews
2 Tbsp. (30 mL) freshly squeezed lemon juice
2 Tbsp. (30 mL) water
2 tsp. (10 mL) freshly ground coarse black
   pepper
1 tsp. (5 mL) kosher or sea salt

Preheat the oven to 375ºF (190ºC).

Place the cashews in a sauté pan over medium–high heat. Cook, stirring constantly, for about 2 minutes or until the cashews are warm but have not changed colour.

Mix the lemon juice and water together and pour over the nuts in the pan. Stir, add the pepper, and continue stirring for about 1 to 2 minutes until the pan is dry.

Remove from heat, toss in the salt, and spoon the nuts in one layer onto a baking pan. Bake for about 8 minutes, shaking pan once or twice. The cashews should be dark golden in colour. Immediately remove to another pan to cool before serving.

Native to Brazil, India, and the West Indies, sweet buttery cashews are the kidney-shaped nut that grows out of the bottom of the cashew apple. Because of their high fat content, they should be stored in the refrigerator.

Bagna Cauda

Bagna Cauda, an Italian peasant dish made with olive oil, garlic, and anchovies, was traditionally served in an earthenware bowl kept warm over coals. When the Bagna Cauda, or dip, was finished, eggs were often scrambled in the same bowl, picking up the residual oil and flavourings. When serving this dish, use the bread to catch the drippings from the dipped vegetables and eat the bread once it is saturated with the oil. Play with the amounts of vegetables and by all means add ones you like and eliminate ones you don't care for.

½ cup (120 mL) good quality virgin olive oil
2½ Tbsp. (37.5 mL) minced anchovy fillets
4 medium to large garlic cloves, very finely minced or grated
1 Tbsp. (15 mL) unsalted butter
1 large handful lightly steamed and cooled green beans
1½ cups (360 mL) lightly steamed and cooled broccoli florets

1½ cups (360 mL) lightly steamed and cooled cauliflower florets
thin batons of carrots from 2 medium carrots
Belgian endive leaves from 1 large endive
batons of zucchini from 1 large zucchini
toasted or grilled baguette, Calabrese, ciabatta, or francese slices

Combine the oil and the anchovies in a small saucepan over low heat until the anchovies have almost dissolved, about 4 to 5 minutes.

Remove from heat and stir in the garlic. Return to heat for about 30 to 45 seconds to just cook the garlic. Remove the pan from heat and stir in the butter.

Transfer the anchovy-garlic mixture to a small, heat-proof dish and place on a large platter over a warmer. Surround with the vegetables and the toasted or grilled crusty bread.

In the Middle Ages garlic was believed to ward off the plague, protect against vampires, and bring good luck.

Lush Madeira-Infused Pâté with Port-Soaked Apricots

MAKES 5 CUPS (1.2 L)

Vaughan Chittock, a gifted New Zealand chef, learned to make a version of this smooth, luxurious pâté when he was an apprentice at a Michelin three-star restaurant in England. He has made some changes to the original recipe and I, in turn, have added a few more chicken livers to the mix. The Port-Soaked Apricots make a good thing even better. Serve with slices of pain au lait, brioche, or baguette. This pâté freezes well so you can avoid the temptation of eating it all at once.

¾ lb. (340 g) chicken livers
½ cup (120 mL) melted unsalted butter
½ tsp. (2.5 mL) kosher salt
½ cup (120 mL) Madeira
2 Tbsp. (30 mL) finely minced shallots
½ tsp. (2.5 mL) finely minced garlic
1 tsp. (5 mL) minced fresh thyme
1 Tbsp. (15 mL) minced fresh Italian parsley

⅛ heaping tsp. (0.5 mL) ground allspice
1 Tbsp. (15 mL) cognac
3 large eggs
2 cups (475 mL) 35% warm cream
slices of pain au lait, brioche, challah (see
    page 17) or baguette
PORT-SOAKED APRICOTS (SEE PAGE 66)

Preheat the oven to 325°F (165°C).

Sauté the chicken livers in 1 Tbsp. (15 mL) melted butter over medium heat for 4 to 5 minutes or until the outsides have turned pale brown but the livers aren't cooked through. Add the salt, Madeira, shallots, garlic, thyme, parsley, and allspice to the pan and bring to a simmer. Continue simmering until the livers are just barely pink in the middle and the liquid in the pan has reduced by about half and is thick and syrupy.

Transfer the sautéed livers to a food processor. Deglaze the hot pan by adding the cognac and scraping up the browned bits from the bottom. Add the deglazed liquid, along with the remaining melted butter and the eggs, to the food processor and pulse until well combined. With the food processor on, slowly pour in the warm cream through the spout in the lid. Blend until smooth. It will be a very loose purée.

Pour the processed mixture through a coarse sieve into a mixing bowl. Once the mixture has been strained, strain again through a finer sieve, into a second mixing bowl. If there is any froth, skim it off. Discard the residue left in the sieve. Pour the strained mixture into five 1-cup (240-mL) ramekins and cover with tin foil. Bake in a *bain marie* (see page 42) for 45 to 50 minutes or until the pâté has set but isn't too hard.

Cool, then cover and refrigerate until ready to serve. Once cooled, the pâté has the consistency of crème brûlée. It will last in the refrigerator for 2 to 3 days or for 1 month in the freezer. Serve with baguette and sliced Port-Soaked Apricots (see page 66).

Port-Soaked Apricots

MAKES 1 GENEROUS CUP (240 mL)

⅓ cup (80 mL) water
½ cup (60 mL) port
⅛ tsp. (0.5 mL) freshly ground black pepper
2 single 4-inch (10-cm) sprigs fresh thyme
¼ tsp. (1.2 mL) honey
1 tsp. (5 mL) balsamic vinegar
1 cup (240 mL) dried apricots

Bring the water, port, pepper, thyme, honey, and vinegar to a simmer in a small saucepan over medium heat. Add the apricots, return to a simmer, and cook for 10 minutes more. Remove from the heat and cool in the liquid for half an hour. Drain the apricots into a bowl and set aside. Return the saucepan to stove top and boil the liquid for 1 minute. Pour over the fruit, toss, and marinate for a few hours before serving.

For a pretty presentation, cut the apricots into ¼-inch (6-mm) slices and place in a small bowl beside the pâté and bread.

COOK'S TIP

Dried apricots are rich in vitamin A, iron, and calcium. Since most dried fruit is treated with sulphur dioxide, you may want to buy organic. Unlike the peachy-orange regular apricots, the colour of organic dried apricots is light brown.

Pain au lait, traditionally used in France for "Croque Monsieur," is a tight-crumbed, soft-crusted but light, white loaf, made with milk, eggs and a touch of sugar. Its flavour, but not its texture, is similar to brioche. For a recipe, see The ACE Bakery Cookbook: Recipes for and with Bread.

Liptauer Cheese Spread

MAKES 1 GENEROUS CUP (240 mL)

When I was in my early twenties, my friend Sandy lived in the apartment below me. She threw great parties and always cooked Slavic food. More often than not, her Liptauer cheese spread was on the table. I like to serve it with drinks before a casual spring dinner, accompanied by radishes and pieces of baguette. You should make this spread the day before serving it as it needs 24 hours to allow the flavours to meld.

½ lb. (225 g) cream cheese
4 Tbsp. (60 mL) mashed feta cheese
2 heaping Tbsp. (30 mL) sour cream or yogurt
1 small garlic clove, finely grated, about ¼
    tsp. (1.2 mL)
1 tsp. (5 mL) finely grated onion

½ tsp. (2.5 mL) hot paprika
1½ tsp. (7.5 mL) sweet paprika
2 Tbsp. (30 mL) minced fresh Italian parsley
1 baguette, sliced or Baguette Flatbread (see
    page 35)
1 to 2 bunches fresh radishes, cleaned

In a medium bowl, mix the cream cheese, feta, and sour cream or yogurt together. Add the garlic, onion, hot and sweet paprika, and parsley; incorporate thoroughly.

Spoon into a serving bowl, cover, and store in the refrigerator for 24 hours.

When ready to eat, return to room temperature and serve with baguette slices and fresh radishes.

COOK'S TIP

Go gently with the garlic—its flavour becomes very pronounced during the 24 hours in the refrigerator.

Ground paprika can be sweet, bittersweet, or hot depending on the heat of the peppers and the amount of seeds and veins ground into the powder.

Mushroom, Roasted Garlic and Chèvre Crostini

MAKES 8 TO 10 CROSTINI

I've used Portobello, button, and shiitake mushrooms for this crostini but you can use any combination you like. They're a great start to a rustic dinner of chili garlic-rubbed roasted Cornish hens with crème fraîche mashed potatoes, or as a light lunch with an endive salad.

1 head garlic
½ tsp. (2.5 mL) good quality virgin olive oil
1 large Portobello mushroom
3 to 4 large white button mushrooms
14 to 16 medium shiitake mushrooms, stems
    removed
1 Tbsp. (15 mL) unsalted butter
1 tsp. (5 mL) minced fresh thyme
kosher salt and freshly ground black pepper,
    to taste

2 slices prosciutto (optional)
2 to 3 generous Tbsp. (30 to 45 mL) chèvre
1 baguette, or Calabrese ring or baguette,
    sliced ½-inch (1.2-cm) thick
up to 1 Tbsp. (15 mL) freshly squeezed lemon
    juice
truffle oil (optional)

Preheat the oven to 375°F (190°C).

Cut the top off the garlic head so it is flat. Place the garlic on a piece of tin foil large enough to wrap it completely. Drizzle with olive oil and wrap it tightly. Roast in the oven for about 1 hour or until the garlic is soft.

Meanwhile, scoop out the black gill from the Portobello mushroom with a teaspoon and discard, along with the stem (or keep the stem for vegetable stock). Cut the mushroom into ⅛-inch (3-mm) slices, then each slice into thirds. Slice the button and shiitake mushrooms into ⅛-inch (3-mm) pieces.

Melt the butter in a frying pan and sauté the mushrooms over medium heat until almost cooked. Mix in the thyme, salt, and pepper, and continue sautéing until the mushrooms are cooked but still plump. Set aside.

Hold the still-warm garlic head cut-side down, and squeeze the roasted, soft garlic cloves into a bowl.

Tear the prosciutto into strips approximately 3 inches × ½ inch (7.5 × 1.2 cm). Break the chèvre into ¼- to ½-inch (6-mm to 1.2-cm) clumps.

Grill or toast the bread. Reheat the mushrooms and stir in some lemon juice. Spread a layer of roasted garlic over the bread and spoon on a mound of mushrooms. Sprinkle with a few drops of truffle oil (if using) and top with either a chunk of chèvre or a curl of prosciutto. Serve warm.

COOK'S TIP

Roasted garlic heads are a great kitchen staple. Whisk into mayonnaise and use as a dip for French fries, mix with fresh horseradish and unsweetened whipped cream to serve with roast beef, or stir into mashed potatoes. The cooked bulbs will keep in the refrigerator for up to a week.

Red Pepper Butter and Feta Crostini
p. 70

Roman Artichoke Crostini
p. 72

Mushroom, Roasted Garlic
and Chèvre Crostini

Red Pepper Butter and Feta Crostini

MAKES 10 CROSTINI (WITH RED PEPPER BUTTER TO SPARE)

While doing a book signing in Detroit for the first ACE Bakery cookbook, an elderly Italian woman came up to me and asked if I had tasted red pepper butter (see page 71). She proceeded to tell me that she had it on toast for breakfast, on sandwiches for lunch and sometimes spooned over roasted chicken for dinner. Slowly cooked red peppers, melted into a purée, are the foundation for this easy to put together crostini. If you've made the "butter" a day or two ahead, you can assemble this treat in less than 15 minutes (photo page 69).

10 Tbsp. (150 mL) warm Red Pepper Butter
   (see recipe opposite)
ten ¾-inch (1.9-cm) slices white baguette,
   or Calabrese ring or baguette
1 Tbsp. (15 mL) olive oil
¼ cup (60 mL) crumbled feta
1 Tbsp. (15 mL) finely chopped basil or Italian
   parsley

Warm the Red Pepper Butter. Grill or toast the baguette or Calabrese slices and brush one side with olive oil.

Generously spread about 1 Tbsp. (15 mL) warmed Red Pepper Butter on each slice of bread. Top each with crumbled feta and a sprinkling of either basil or parsley or both.

Serve while the Red Pepper Butter is still warm.

Bell peppers can be green, purple, brown, yellow, orange, or red. Red bell peppers are just green peppers that have ripened on the vine for a longer time.

Red Pepper Butter

MAKES 2 CUPS (475 ML)

Red Pepper Butter will keep in the refrigerator for weeks. It's scrumptious spread on a sandwich piled high with grilled vegetables and is a perfect accompaniment to grilled fish or chicken. Don't be put off by the long cooking period—most of the time the peppers can be left unattended.

10 red medium to large red bell peppers
4 Tbsp. (60 mL) olive oil
1½ generous tsp. (7.5 mL) finely minced
   garlic

Preheat the oven to broil.

Place the peppers on a baking tray and broil each side for approximately 4 to 5 minutes or until the skin starts to blister and blacken. Remove from the oven and cool before peeling the skin off the peppers. Remove seeds and coarsely chop the peppers.

Pour the olive oil into a sauté pan and heat on medium until just warm. Add the peppers and turn the heat to medium-low. Cook the peppers for 90 minutes, stirring occasionally to prevent them from burning, or until they start to fall apart.

Stir in the minced garlic and cook for another 15 to 20 minutes, stirring a few times, until the peppers have the consistency of purée.

Cool and store, covered, in the refrigerator until ready to use.

COOK'S TIP

Place the roasted peppers in a paper bag and seal it shut. Leave for 15 minutes to allow the heat to loosen the skins, making the peppers easier to peel.

Roman Artichoke Crostini

MAKES 10 TO 12 CROSTINI

Marinated artichokes from various companies will taste different depending on the ingredients in the marinades. For a zesty topping, simply drain the artichokes, but for a more subtle but truer artichoke taste, rinse the artichoke hearts before using (photo page 69).

6-oz. (170-mL) jar of marinated artichokes, rinsed and drained
4 to 5 Tbsp. (60 to 75 mL) mascarpone
½ medium garlic clove, grated
1 Tbsp. (15 mL) or more freshly squeezed lemon juice

1 Tbsp. (15 mL) minced fresh chives
white, Calabrese or sourdough baguette, sliced ½-inch (1.2-cm) thick
1 to 2 Tbsp. (15 to 30 mL) extra-virgin olive oil

Roughly purée the artichokes, mascarpone, and garlic in a food processor. Mix in 1 Tbsp. (15 mL) lemon juice. Taste and add more lemon juice if needed. The finished purée should have some texture and not be completely smooth. Transfer to a bowl and fold in the chives.

Toast or grill the bread and drizzle one side with olive oil. Mound with the artichoke purée while the bread is still warm.

Fall Vegetable Crostini

Erin Marcus, our Foodservice Manager, created this recipe for an event that raised funds for organic farming. The roasted cherry tomato adds a burst of colour and a fresh tangy taste.

20 cherry tomatoes
6 to 7 Tbsp. (90 to 105 mL) good quality olive oil
kosher salt and freshly ground white pepper
1 tsp. (5 mL) kosher salt
1 medium to large head of cauliflower, cut into florets
2 tsp. (10 mL) curry powder

2 tsp. (10 mL) cumin powder
⅓ cup (80 mL) freshly grated Parmigiano Reggiano
up to ¼ cup (60 mL) extra-virgin olive oil
1 tsp. (5 mL) freshly squeezed lemon juice, or to taste
twenty ½-inch (1.2-cm) slices baguette, toasted

Preheat the oven to 350°F (175°C).

Slice the tomatoes in half and place in a bowl. Drizzle with 2 to 3 Tbsp. (30 to 45 mL) olive oil and season with salt and pepper. Toss gently to coat the tomatoes in a thin layer of oil. Spoon them in a single layer onto a baking pan. Bake for 10 to 15 minutes or until the tomatoes have softened but not collapsed. Remove from the heat and set aside.

In a large pot, bring 4 to 5 cups (950 mL to 1.2 L) water to a rapid boil. Add 1 tsp. (5 mL) salt and the cauliflower florets. Cook until the florets can be pierced with a fork but offer a little resistance. Remove from the pot and drain for 15 minutes.

Toss cauliflower florets in a bowl with just enough olive oil to lightly coat, about 2 to 3 tsp. (10 to 15 mL). Sprinkle the curry and cumin over the cauliflower and toss again. Season with salt and pepper to taste.

Place on a baking sheet and roast in the oven for 15 to 20 minutes. Rotate florets after 10 minutes. Remove early if cauliflower begins to turn colour.

Transfer the cauliflower to a food processor. Add the cheese and 1 to 2 Tbsp. (15 to 30 mL) of extra-virgin olive oil while the processor is on to create a smooth, velvety texture. Dribble in more oil if necessary.

Add lemon juice, and salt and pepper to taste.

Serve mounded on toasted baguette slices. Top each crostini with two roasted cherry tomato halves.

Baguette Flatbread p. 35

Tuscan Pesto

MAKES 2½ CUPS (600 ML)

A wonderful Tuscan cook was kind enough to tell me what he used in his fabulous pesto. Walnuts and white wine vinegar are his secret ingredients. This interpretation of his recipe can be used in many ways. Try it in Pasta al Pesto (see page 156), as a nibble on grilled baguette, or as a spread mixed with mayonnaise on the Chicken Club for a Crowd (see page 119).

⅓ cup (80 mL) pine nuts
¼ cup (60 mL) packed walnut halves
14 to 15 cups (3.5 to 3.75 L) loosely packed fresh basil leaves, about 5 large bunches
3 cups (720 mL) loosely packed Italian parsley, large stalks removed, about 1 large bunch
2 medium to large garlic cloves, roughly chopped

3½ oz. (100 g) freshly grated Parmigiano Reggiano
¾ to 1 cup (180 to 240 mL) extra-virgin olive oil
2 Tbsp. (30 mL) white wine vinegar
¼ tsp. (1.2 mL) kosher salt

Preheat the oven to 375°F (190°C).

On a baking sheet, toast the pine nuts and walnuts in the oven for 3 minutes. Remove toasted nuts from oven and let cool before roughly chopping.

Wash and dry the basil and parsley. In a food processor, put in as much basil and parsley as possible before adding the pine nuts, walnuts, garlic, and cheese. Pour in half the olive oil and all of the vinegar and pulse, adding more herbs and more oil as the volume decreases. Don't over-process. The pesto should have some texture and not be completely smooth. Add more oil if the pesto is too thick.

Taste and add salt if necessary before transferring to a serving bowl.

COOK'S TIP
The pesto will keep, covered in the refrigerator, for 3 to 4 days and in the freezer for 2 months. Although the top layer will turn darker, just mix it into the green pesto.

Basil, a member of the mint family, has a slightly peppery flavour. There are many different types of basil used in cooking around the world. Sweet and bush basil are generally used in Western cooking while a variety of basils, including Thai, licorice, lemon, and holy basil, are used in Asian dishes.

Sun-Dried Tomato Pesto

MAKES ⅔ CUP (160 mL)

This recipe forms quite a dense pesto, best for spreading on sandwiches. If you plan to use this as a sauce for pasta, you may wish to use more of the reserved oil.

6¾-oz. (202-mL) jar sun-dried tomatoes,
   in oil
1½ Tbsp. (22.5 mL) drained capers
¼ cup (60 mL) loosely packed, roughly
   julienned fresh basil
¼ tsp. (1.2 mL) loosely packed, chopped fresh
   rosemary

Drain the tomatoes and reserve the oil.

In a small food processor, add the tomatoes, capers, basil, rosemary and 1 Tbsp. plus 1 tsp. (20 mL) of the reserved oil. Pulse until ingredients are well combined. (If the pesto is too thick, add more oil and pulse briefly.)

The pesto will keep, covered in the refrigerator, for 3 to 4 weeks.

Capers, a member of the cabbage family, are the unopened flower buds of a Mediterranean bush called *Capparis spinosa*. The bud, used as a sour-salty accent in recipes, can be preserved in a variety of ways: dry-salted, in vinegar, or in brine.

Spiced Pear Ketchup

MAKES ¾ CUP (180 mL)

I came up with this ketchup to accompany the ACE Grilled Blue Cheese, Parmigiano Reggiano and Bresaola Sandwich (see page 118). It's equally good spread on multigrain bread with roast pork and grilled zucchini or as a dip for sweet potato fries.

1 Tbsp. (15 mL) unsalted butter	4-inch (10-cm) sprig of fresh rosemary, leaves
2 Bosc or other cooking pears, peeled, cored,	only, very finely minced
and cut into 1-inch (2.5-cm) chunks	2½ Tbsp. (37.5 mL) pear vinegar
1 Tbsp. (15 mL) finely minced cooking onion	1 tsp. (5 mL) raw sugar
½ tsp. (2.5 mL) kosher salt	1 large star anise
⅛ tsp. (0.5 mL) freshly ground white pepper	1 small bay leaf

In a small sauté pan or frying pan over medium heat, melt the butter and sauté the pears for 2 minutes. Add the onion and continue sautéing for another 5 to 7 minutes or until the pears have softened but not turned colour.

Remove from the heat and let cool. Place cooled pears in a food processor with the salt, pepper, rosemary, vinegar, and sugar and purée. Return the mixture to the sauté pan, add the star anise and the bay leaf, and simmer for approximately 5 to 10 minutes or until the mixture thickens to the consistency of ketchup.

Remove ketchup from heat and let cool for 1 to 2 hours. Discard bay leaf and star anise and taste—if the pears used were very sweet, you may want to add another ½ Tbsp. (7.5 mL) of vinegar.

Spiced Pear Ketchup will keep refrigerated for 6 weeks and frozen for 6 months.

Many food historians believe ketchup originated in Malaysia, where it contained pickled fish and spices. It wasn't until the early 1800s that British and North American cookbooks noted the addition of tomatoes.

Soups

Baked Eggplant Soup with Feta-Mint Garnish   80

Tomato, Ginger and Orange Soup with Mini Croutons   81

Roasted Beet and Apple Purée with Crème Fraîche   82

Red Pepper and Corn Soup   84

Sorrel Soup with Grilled Salmon   85

African Papaya Soup   87

Moroccan Chicken Lentil Stew   88

Pappa al Pomodoro   91

Roasted Mushroom, Pancetta and Thyme Potage   92

*"Only the pure of heart
can make a good soup."
—Ludwig van Beethoven*

Baked Eggplant Soup with Feta-Mint Garnish

MAKES 9 TO 10 CUPS (2.1 TO 2.4 L)

We have been making this soup at our café since the doors opened over 10 years ago. Although you can make it with a minimum of fuss or time, it has a wonderful, smooth texture and gentle flavour that has made it a favourite with our customers. The feta-mint garnish added by our daughter, Devin, not only looks pretty but also adds a little taste surprise.

2 large eggplants
4 cloves medium to large garlic, peeled and sliced in quarters
⅓ cup (80 mL) good quality virgin olive oil, for brushing eggplant and sautéing vegetables
2 Tbsp. (30 mL) unsalted butter
3 small yellow cooking onions, sliced ¼-inch (6-mm) thick
2 oz. (57 g) leek, cleaned, sliced in ¼-inch (6-mm) rings (white part only), about ½ cup (120 mL)

2 medium to large celery stalks, sliced ½-inch (1.2-cm) thick
1 tsp. (5 mL) ground cumin
1 medium Yukon Gold potato, peeled and cut into ½-inch (1.2-cm) cubes
6 to 7 cups (1.5 to 1.7 L) vegetable stock
1 to 2 tsp. (5 to 10 mL) freshly squeezed lemon juice
kosher salt and freshly ground black pepper, to taste
crumbled feta and julienned fresh mint, for garnish

Preheat the oven to 350°F (175°C).

Cut eggplants in half, lengthwise. Score the flesh and insert slices of garlic into the cuts. Brush with a little olive oil and season with salt and pepper. Place, skin-side down, on a baking sheet and bake until soft, about one hour. Remove from the heat and set aside.

In a pot large enough to hold all the ingredients, heat the remaining olive oil and butter over medium heat. When the butter has melted, add onions, leek, and celery. Cover and sweat for about 10 minutes, until onion is translucent and the leeks and celery are softened but not browned. Sprinkle in the cumin and cook a minute longer. Add the potato and 2 cups (475 mL) of stock. Bring to a boil. Reduce heat to low and simmer 20 minutes or until the potato is tender.

Scoop the garlic and the flesh out of the eggplants and add to the soup along with 3 cups (720 mL) of stock. Cook for another 5 minutes. Remove from heat and cool before puréeing in batches with a hand blender or in a blender or food processor. Use the remaining vegetable stock to adjust the consistency of the purée, and add lemon juice, salt, and pepper to taste.

Return purée to stove and heat up before ladling into bowls. Top with crumbled feta and fresh mint before serving.

Eggplant, a member of the nightshade family, is related to the tomato and potato. Look for smooth-skinned eggplants that seem heavy for their size, with no soft or brown spots.

Tomato, Ginger and Orange Soup with Mini Croutons

MAKES 8 CUPS (2 L)

Tomato and ginger may seem like an unlikely pairing but the spicy sweet taste of the ginger balances perfectly with the acidity of the tomatoes. A touch of orange juice melds the flavours. Play around with the amount of orange juice, depending on the sweetness of the tomatoes. Tomato and ginger should be the dominant flavours.

3 Tbsp. (45 mL) vegetable oil
1 medium yellow cooking onion, diced
five ⅛-inch (3-mm) peeled slices fresh ginger
 (see Cook's Tips)
4 garlic cloves minced
2 bay leaves
two 28-oz (796-mL) cans whole tomatoes
 in juice
3 cups (720 mL) vegetable stock

½ to 1 cup (120 to 240 mL) freshly squeezed
 orange juice, pulp removed
kosher salt and freshly ground black pepper,
 to taste
2 Tbsp. (30 mL) unsalted butter
2 large slices white, Calabrese, or sourdough
 bread, crusts removed and cut into ¼-inch
 (6-mm) croutons
lightly whipped cream for garnish

Heat vegetable oil on medium-high for 30 seconds in a pot large enough to hold all the ingredients. Add the onion, lower the heat to medium-low, and sauté, stirring occasionally, for about 5 to 7 minutes or until the onions are translucent but not browned. Add ginger and sauté for 1 minute. Add garlic and bay leaves and sauté another 30 seconds.

Pour in tomatoes with their juice and the stock. Bring to a low boil and then simmer partially covered for 20 to 25 minutes. Remove from heat and stir in ½ cup (120 mL) orange juice. Let cool before puréeing in batches with a hand blender, or in a blender or food processor. Add salt and pepper to taste. More finely grated ginger can be added if you want a stronger ginger taste; if you want a more pronounced orange flavour, add the remaining orange juice.

Melt the butter over medium-high heat in a frying pan, add croutons, and sauté until golden brown. Drain on a paper towel.

Heat soup, ladle into bowls, and top each serving with a generous dollop of lightly whipped cream and some croutons.

COOK'S TIPS

1. Make sure you make very small croutons; large ones will overpower the soup's texture.

2. A soup spoon is the perfect utensil to peel fresh ginger. Just scrape the tip of the spoon forcefully down the side of the root. The skin will "peel" off.

Roasted Beet and Apple Purée with Crème Fraîche

MAKES 11 CUPS (2.6 L)

I find that beets and apples have a natural affinity, whether mashed together to make a purée to eat with lamb chops, or as a soup topped with a swirl of crème fraîche. All the ingredients in this recipe, except for the stock, of course, are roasted in the oven. Once done, just purée everything together and it's ready to eat. Crème fraîche is available in most supermarkets, but I have included a homemade recipe if you are in the mood to make your own. Five minutes of prep will be needed the day before you plan to use it.

2 lbs. (900 g) beets, stemmed and scrubbed (about 3 bunches)
2 medium yellow cooking onions, peeled and halved
2 Granny Smith apples, unpeeled, halved and cored
2 medium to large garlic cloves, peeled
2 medium carrots, stemmed and washed
2 bay leaves
1 tsp. (5 mL) vegetable oil

2 tsp. (10 mL) raspberry vinegar
4 cups (950 mL) beef stock, plus ½ cup (120 mL) more if needed
kosher salt and freshly ground black pepper, to taste
crème fraîche, good quality store-bought (or see below)

HOMEMADE CRÈME FRAÎCHE
1 cup (240 mL) 35% cream
¼ cup (60 mL) buttermilk

Preheat the oven to 375°F (190°C).

Wrap the beets in tin foil and roast for 35 minutes.

In a large bowl, thoroughly toss the onions, apples, garlic, carrots, and bay leaves in the vegetable oil. Wrap tossed vegetables in tin foil, and place in the oven with the beets and roast for another 45 minutes.

Remove the beets from the oven, cool slightly, and peel (the peel should slip off quite easily). Cut into chunks. Discard the bay leaves and place half of all the roasted vegetables, as well as half the vinegar and 2 cups (475 mL) of stock in a blender or food processor. Purée until smooth. Repeat with the rest of the vegetables and vinegar and another 2 cups (475 mL) of stock. If the soup is too thick, pour in a bit more stock. Season with salt and pepper to taste and serve, heated, in individual bowls topped with crème fraîche.

FOR CRÈME FRAÎCHE

Whisk the cream and buttermilk together in a wide-mouthed bowl. Cover with a towel and leave at room temperature until it becomes as thick as softly whipped cream, about 12 to 24 hours. Cover with plastic wrap and refrigerate until ready to use. Crème fraîche will keep in the refrigerator for 5 to 7 days.

COOK'S TIP
Although you can freeze this soup, freezing diminishes the delicate flavour of the apples.

Zucchini, Carrot and Gruyère Loaf p. 15

Red Pepper and Corn Soup

MAKES 8 TO 10 CUPS (2 TO 2.4 L)

This soup, a summer and autumn favourite at ACE, is best made a few hours ahead, as the flavours take time to develop. I prefer a rough purée as it allows the fresh taste of the peppers and corn to shine. A green salad, a piece of Camembert or St. Andre and a few slices of Flax Bread with Honey and Oats (see page 24) would make a lovely lunch.

4 large red bell peppers, seeded and cut into
  ½-inch (1.2-cm) chunks
4½ cups (1.1 L) fresh or frozen corn
2 to 3 tsp. (10 to 15 mL) vegetable oil
2 small yellow cooking onions, chopped
2 medium stalks celery, chopped
2 leeks, white and light green parts sliced
  ¼-inch (6-mm) thick

2 large garlic cloves, chopped
8 cups (1.7 L) water or 4 cups (950 mL) water
  + 4 cups (950 mL) vegetable stock
½ tsp. (2.5 mL) minced fresh thyme
½ tsp. (2.5 mL) minced fresh rosemary
⅛ tsp. (0.5 mL) cayenne pepper
kosher salt and freshly ground black pepper,
  to taste

Finely mince ¼ cup (60 mL) of red pepper, and reserve, along with ¼ cup (60 mL) corn for garnish.

Heat the vegetable oil over medium heat in a pot large enough to hold all the ingredients. Add the onion, celery, leek, and garlic; cover to sweat, stirring occasionally, until the vegetables have begun to soften but not brown, about 6 to 7 minutes.

Add the remaining red peppers and enough water to just cover the vegetables, about 4 cups (950 mL). Cover and simmer for 30 to 40 minutes or until the peppers are soft. Add the remaining corn, water or stock, and the thyme, rosemary, and cayenne; simmer for another 5 minutes. Using a hand blender, or in a blender or food processor, roughly purée the soup in batches and season with salt and pepper.

When ready to serve, top each bowl with a sprinkling of corn and red pepper.

"A light wind swept over the corn, and all nature laughed in the sunshine."
—Anne Brontë

Sorrel Soup with Grilled Salmon

MAKES 10 CUPS (2.4 L)

Sorrel, a perennial herb, has long thin leaves that range from dark to pale green in colour. Its slightly sour taste makes a perfect accompaniment to rich fish such as salmon. Although spring and summer is the best time to find it, you can buy sorrel in gourmet fruit and vegetable stores throughout the winter. I tend to make large batches of this soup when sorrel is most plentiful and freeze what I don't use for a treat in the depth of winter.

2 small leeks, white and light green part
1 Tbsp. (15 mL) unsalted butter
8 cups (2 L) chicken stock
4 medium white potatoes, peeled and cut into
    1-inch (2.5-cm) pieces
14 oz. (400 g) sorrel
½ tsp. (2.5 mL) granulated sugar
kosher salt and freshly ground white pepper,
    to taste

two 6 oz. (170 g) skinless salmon fillets,
    1½-inch (3.8-cm) thick
1 to 2 tsp. (5 to 10 mL) vegetable oil
kosher salt and freshly ground black pepper for
    the salmon
¼ cup (60 mL) 35% cream, for garnish
salmon eggs

Cut the white and light green parts of the leeks into thin slices and submerge in cold water for a few minutes to clean. Drain and pat dry. Melt the butter in a frying pan and add the leeks. Sauté for about 5 minutes over medium heat or until softened but not browned.

Pour the stock into a pot large enough to hold all the ingredients. Add the leeks and potatoes. Cover and simmer about 15 to 20 minutes or until the potatoes are almost fully cooked. Throw in the sorrel and simmer for another 5 minutes. Remove from the heat, stir in the sugar and, when cool enough, purée in batches with a hand blender or in a blender or food processor. Add salt and white pepper to taste but bear in mind that you will be topping the soup with salmon eggs, which are salty.

Brush the salmon with oil and sprinkle with salt and black pepper. Place a cast iron pan over high heat for 1 to 2 minutes until the base of the pan is very hot. Sear the salmon in the hot pan for 1½ to 2 minutes on each side. Let cool, then break into 10 pieces. The salmon will be very rare but it will get an extra bit of cooking when immersed in the hot soup.

Return soup to medium-low heat.

While soup is reheating, whip the cream into light peaks and place your bowls in a warm oven.

Place 1 piece of salmon in each heated bowl and ladle the soup over the fish. Decorate with a dollop of whipped cream and a sprinkle of salmon eggs over top. Serve immediately.

COOK'S TIP
If you're feeling extravagant, add ¼ cup (60 mL) 18% or 35% cream to the soup before reheating.

African Papaya Soup

MAKES 10 CUPS (2.4 L)

I first had papaya soup when we went to visit our son, Luke, who was spending six months volunteering at a refugee camp in Uganda. I had expected it to be cloyingly sweet but it wasn't. Delicious both hot and cold, depending on the weather, it makes an unusual start to a sophisticated dinner. Make it when the fruit is in season from early spring to late fall. A ripe papaya will give slightly to the touch.

4 Tbsp. (60 mL) corn oil
1 medium yellow cooking onion, peeled and diced, about 1 cup (240 mL)
4 large cloves garlic, peeled and minced
1 tsp. (5 mL) minced fresh ginger
½ tsp. (2.5 mL) curry powder
8 cups (2 L) water
1 medium carrot, peeled and cut into 1-inch (2.5-cm) chunks

1 to 4 ripe papayas (depending on type), peeled, seeded, and cut into 1-inch (2.5-cm) chunks, about 8 cups (2 L)
kosher salt and freshly ground white pepper, to taste
yogurt, freshly ground black pepper and lime zest for garnish

Place the oil and onion in a large pot and sauté over medium heat until the onion is translucent but not browned, about 5 minutes. Add the garlic, ginger, and curry powder, and sauté for 30 seconds, stirring constantly to keep the garlic from burning.

Add the water and carrot to the pot, cover, and bring to a simmer for 30 minutes to make a very light stock.

Remove the carrot from the stock and add the papaya chunks. Simmer for 2 to 3 minutes more, just to heat the fruit.

Purée with a hand blender or in a blender or food processor and season with salt and pepper. Serve warm or at room temperature, garnished with a dollop of yogurt, a sprinkle of black pepper, and a few strands of lime zest.

A papaya can weigh from 1 to 10 pounds (500 g to 4.5 kg). Its skin can range in colour from golden yellow to dark green while its flesh can be yellow, orange, pink, or red, depending on the variety. Papaya trees can be male, female or hermaphrodite, although only the female and hermaphrodite trees produce fruit.

Moroccan Chicken Lentil Stew

MAKES 10 TO 12 CUPS (2.5 TO 2.8 L)

This thick one-dish stew is a cinch to make and can be ready in no time if you use store-bought roasted chicken. If you want a vegetarian stew, just leave out the meat and save yourself a step. Ginger, turmeric, and cinnamon, used in Moroccan savoury dishes, add a warm note to the lentils and chickpeas. All you need is a green salad and good bread to have a satisfying lunch or a casual Sunday supper. Red wine or beer will complete the meal.

2 Tbsp. (30 mL) unsalted butter
2 small yellow cooking onions, chopped
2 large stalks celery, chopped
¾ tsp. (4 mL) ground ginger
½ tsp. (2.5 mL) turmeric
¼ tsp. (1.2 mL) ground cinnamon
2 scant tsp. (10 mL) kosher salt
¼ tsp. (1.2 mL) freshly ground black pepper
1 cup (240 mL) dry green lentils
6 ½ cups (1.6 L) water
2 cups (475 mL) canned crushed tomatoes
  in liquid

1 medium red- or white-skinned potato, peeled
  and cut in ½-inch (1.2-cm) chunks
1 cup (240 mL) chopped ½-inch (1.2-cm)
  pieces of peeled carrot
one 19-oz. (532-mL) can chickpeas, drained
  and rinsed
1 large roasted single chicken breast, skin
  removed and shredded (see Cook's Tip)
⅓ cup (80 mL) chopped fresh coriander
juice of 1 to 2 limes

Put the butter, onion, and celery in a large pot. Turn the heat to medium–low and cook, covered but stirring occasionally, until the vegetables have begun to soften, about 10 to 12 minutes.

Stir in the ginger, turmeric, cinnamon, salt, pepper and lentils. Continue stirring until well mixed together.

Pour the water and the crushed tomatoes into the pot and bring to a boil. Reduce the heat to low and simmer, partly covered, for about 15 minutes, stirring occasionally. Add the potato and carrot and continue simmering, partly covered, for another 10 minutes or until the lentils are tender. Add the chickpeas and chicken, and simmer until they are heated through and the potatoes and carrots are cooked, about 5 minutes longer.

Spoon into bowls and garnish with coriander and a squeeze of lime.

COOK'S TIP

Chunks of chicken won't work in this dish: shredded is best. Take the skin off the roasted chicken and use your hands to pull the meat away from the bone in large strands. This will be easier to do if the chicken is slightly warm or at room temperature.

Rosemary Olive Oil Grissini p. 26

Pappa al Pomodoro

MAKES 7 CUPS (1.7 L)

You will find recipes for this soup in most Italian cookbooks. What differentiates this one is the amount of fresh herbs and the dusting of Parmigiano Reggiano. What I like is that I can have it on the table in a half hour. If you want to purée the whole thing, that's fine too, although I tend to serve the chunky, rustic version.

3 Tbsp. (45 mL) + 2 tsp. (10 mL) olive oil
1 medium yellow cooking onion, chopped, about 1 cup (240 mL)
1 large bay leaf
1 medium to large garlic clove, minced
3½ cups (840 mL) fresh or day-old white bread, crusts on, cut into ½-inch (1.2-cm) cubes
1 cup (240 mL) water or vegetable stock
1½ Tbsp. (22.5 mL) coarsely chopped fresh oregano

1½ tsp. (7.5 mL) coarsely chopped fresh thyme
two 28-oz. (796-mL) cans tomatoes in liquid, drained and roughly chopped. Reserve liquid
3 cups (720 mL) juice from canned tomatoes
½ tsp. (2.5 mL) kosher salt
freshly ground black pepper, to taste
large pinch granulated sugar
⅓ cup (80 mL) grated Parmigiano Reggiano

In a pot large enough to hold all the ingredients, gently heat 3 Tbsp. (45 mL) olive oil and add the chopped onion and bay leaf. Sauté, stirring, over medium heat until the onions are light golden in colour, about 5 minutes. Add garlic and sauté one minute longer, making sure the garlic doesn't burn. Add 2 cups (475 mL) of the bread cubes and cook until bread has absorbed the oil and is lightly toasted.

Add the stock, herbs, tomatoes, and tomato juice. Adjust heat so that the soup simmers for 10 minutes. Stir occasionally and gently, taking care not to break up the bread cubes.

Meanwhile, heat the remaining 2 tsp. (10 mL) olive oil over medium heat and sauté the remaining 1½ cups (360 mL) bread cubes until crisp, about 4 to 5 minutes; set aside.

Remove the soup from heat and season with salt, pepper, and sugar. Discard the bay leaf.

Ladle into bowls and serve topped with a few toasted bread cubes and a sprinkling of grated Parmigiano Reggiano.

Roasted Mushroom, Pancetta and Thyme Potage

MAKES 5 TO 6 CUPS (1.2 TO 1.5 L)

Roasted mushrooms, which have a more intense flavour than sautéed mushrooms, are the secret to this full-flavoured soup. Pancetta—Italian bacon cured with spices and salt but not smoked—adds just the right degree of richness. If you can't find pancetta, substitute thickly cut smoked bacon. The taste will be slightly different but still satisfying. Serve with dense whole-wheat or multigrain rolls or Baguette Flatbreads (see page 35).

13 oz. (370 g) button mushrooms, sliced ⅛-inch (3-mm) thick
7 oz. (200 g) shiitake mushrooms, stems off, sliced ¼-inch (6-mm) thick
4 Tbsp. + 2 tsp. (70 mL) olive oil
¼ heaping tsp. (5 mL) kosher salt
2 heaping tsp. (10 mL) finely minced garlic
¼ heaping tsp. (1.2 mL) finely minced fresh thyme

1 small yellow cooking onion, finely chopped
two ¼-inch thick (6-mm) slices pancetta, cut in ½-inch (1.2-cm) squares
3 Tbsp. (45 mL) Madeira
4 cups (950 mL) chicken stock, + ½ cup (120 mL) if needed
freshly ground black pepper, to taste
¼ cup (60 mL) 35% cream
fresh chives, for garnish

Preheat the oven to 375°F (190°C).

In an oven-proof dish, toss the mushrooms with 4 Tbsp. (60 mL) olive oil and the salt. Arrange the mushrooms in a fairly flat layer, transfer to oven, and roast for 30 minutes, stirring once or twice. Toss in the garlic and thyme and continue cooking for another 15 minutes.

Meanwhile, put the remaining 2 tsp. (10 mL) olive oil and chopped onion in a small frying pan over medium heat. Sauté the onion until light golden. Remove onion and set aside. In the same pan, sauté the pancetta until it has rendered almost all of its fat. (You may need a bit more oil to get started.) Deglaze the pan by adding 2 Tbsp. (30 mL) Madeira and scraping up any browned bits from the bottom of the pan.

In a soup pot, bring the 4 cups (950 mL) stock to a simmer over medium-high heat. Add the mushrooms and onions, as well as the pancetta and deglazed liquid from the pan. Now is the time to decide if you want a textured or smooth soup. Using a hand blender or in a blender or food processor purée accordingly. Mix in the remaining 1 Tbsp. (15 mL) Madeira and the cream. If the soup is too thick, stir in the extra ½ cup (120 mL) hot stock. Season with freshly ground black pepper.

Serve warm, decorated with 2 or 3 long stalks of chives per bowl.

Although mushrooms have been eaten throughout the world, some countries passed laws forbidding common people to eat them. For those who could eat mushrooms, the more mushroom dishes that were served, the higher their standing in society. In the 1700s, growing mushrooms in garden beds became too expensive for French farmers to maintain. Their mushroom crops were moved to caves created by the quarrying of stone used to construct magnificent buildings in Paris. This is the origin of the term "champignons de Paris" — the common white button mushroom.

Salads

Autumn Chicken Salad   96

Gingered Fennel and Apple Slaw with Buttermilk Dressing   97

Minted Zucchini and Almond Salad   98

Winter Cauliflower and Broccoli Salad   99

Boston Lettuce with Walnuts, Apple and Gruyère
in a Citrus-Mint Vinaigrette   100

Summer Radish, Cucumber and Italian Parsley Salad   103

Arugula, Fig and Chèvre Salad with Red Wine Vinaigrette   104

Cranberry Pecan Wild Rice Salad   105

Israeli Couscous Salad with Spring Pea Mix   106

Warm Roasted Sweet Potato and Pear Salad   109

Enza's Tomatoes Stuffed with Shrimp, Tuna or Egg   110

Brussels Sprouts and Bacon Salad with French Vinaigrette   112

"To make a good salad is to be a brilliant
diplomat — to know how much oil to put
with one's vinegar."

—Oscar Wilde

Autumn Chicken Salad

SERVES 4

This is a wonderful way to use chicken left over from the night before. But I like it so much, I usually roast a chicken just for the pleasure of having more of this salad available. Don't be deceived by the amount of vinaigrette called for. You will need every bit to coat the meat, fruit, and vegetables. For an attractive presentation, serve the salad in a bowl lined with Boston lettuce leaves. If you're looking for a light, easy, do-ahead, late-summer dinner, start with African Papaya Soup (see page 87), serve the salad with warm focaccia, and finish off with the Ice Cream Surprise Cake (see page 192).

VINAIGRETTE

3 Tbsp. (45 mL) minced shallots
3 Tbsp. (45 mL) freshly squeezed lemon juice
1½ Tbsp. (22.5 mL) freshly squeezed orange juice
½ tsp. (2.5 mL) kosher salt
2 tsp. (10 mL) Dijon mustard
4 Tbsp. (60 mL) walnut oil
3 Tbsp. (45 mL) vegetable oil
½ tsp. (2.5 mL) minced fresh rosemary

SALAD

2 large chicken breasts, cooked, skinned and shredded (see Cook's Tip page 88)
2 Tbsp. (30 mL) golden raisins
24 prunes, cut in quarters
⅔ cup (160 mL) ¼-inch (6-mm) diced celery
1 Granny Smith apple, peeled, cored and julienned
½ cup (120 mL) walnut halves, coarsely broken
kosher salt and freshly ground black pepper to taste
1½ Tbsp. (22.5 mL) minced fresh chives
2 Tbsp. (30 mL) minced Italian parsley

FOR THE VINAIGRETTE

In a small bowl, whisk together the shallots, lemon and orange juice, and kosher salt. Let sit for 10 minutes. Whisk in the mustard and then both oils. Add the rosemary, whisk once more, and set aside.

FOR THE SALAD

Put the shredded chicken, raisins, prunes, celery, apple, and walnuts in a serving bowl. Toss with the vinaigrette, season with salt and pepper, and sprinkle with chives and parsley.

COOK'S TIP

Lightly spray your knife with vegetable oil to prevent prunes from adhering to the knife as you slice. Alternatively, spray clean kitchen scissors with vegetable oil and cut the prunes in pieces.

Gingered Fennel and Apple Slaw with Buttermilk Dressing

SERVES 6 TO 8

Both buttermilk and lemon keep the apple in this salad from turning brown so you have the luxury of making it several hours before serving it. It will stay crisp for 2 to 3 hours. Try serving it with pork burgers or even barbecued pork tenderloin. It's also great with the Chicken Club for a Crowd (see page 119). To me, either combo is reason enough for a picnic.

1 large fennel bulb with fronds attached
2 Granny Smith apples, peeled and cored
4 to 5 paper-thin slices sweet white onion, soaked in cold water for 20 minutes, drained and patted dry
¼ cup (60 mL) sour cream
¼ cup (60 mL) buttermilk

1 tsp. (5 mL) grated fresh ginger or more to taste
1 Tbsp. (15 mL) freshly squeezed lemon juice
½ tsp. kosher salt
5 grinds coarsely ground black pepper
⅓ to ½ cup (80 to 120 mL) coarsely chopped Italian parsley

Cut the fronds off the fennel bulb and reserve for garnish.

Thinly julienne the fennel and apples on a mandoline or in a food processor. Place in a bowl and add the onion slices.

In a small bowl, whisk together the sour cream, buttermilk, ginger, lemon juice, kosher salt, and pepper.

Toss the dressing in with the vegetable mixture. Add the parsley and toss again. Top with a few fennel fronds before serving.

COOK'S TIP

Although fresh ginger will keep in the crisper of your refrigerator for up to two weeks, it can be frozen if tightly wrapped. Cut off what you need and return the rest to the freezer. See Cook's Tips, page 81, for how to peel ginger.

Minted Zucchini and Almond Salad

SERVES 4 TO 6

Mint and lemon zest partner well with the delicate taste of zucchini. I find this versatile salad tastes wonderful with grilled fish or cold-roasted chicken. I also like it as part of a picnic that includes the Roasted Portobello with Herbed Cheeses on Baguette (see page 122), Oatmeal Shortbread (see page 190), and a bowl of cherries. If you are picnicking, carry the vinaigrette separately and dress the zucchini at the last moment.

¼ cup (60 mL) almond slivers, not flakes
5 medium, unpeeled zucchini, washed and stemmed
1 Tbsp. (15 mL) rice vinegar
1 Tbsp. + 1 tsp. (20 mL) safflower oil
¾ tsp. (4 mL) lemon zest

2 tsp. (10 mL) finely chopped fresh mint
large pinch kosher salt
pinch granulated sugar
freshly ground black pepper
2 tsp. (10 mL) finely minced green onion
⅛ tsp. (0.5 mL) chili powder (optional)

Preheat the oven to 350°F (175°C) and toast the almonds on a baking sheet for 5 minutes or until golden.

Using a mandoline or a vegetable peeler, cut the zucchini in paper-thin slices, lengthwise. Shock the zucchini slices in a pot of boiling water for 30 seconds to 1 minute, until just softened. They will become flexible. Immediately plunge into cold water to stop the cooking process, and, once cool, drain and thoroughly pat dry with paper towels.

In a small bowl, combine the vinegar, oil, lemon zest, mint, salt, sugar, and pepper, and whisk together to make the dressing.

Gently toss the zucchini, almonds, and green onions in a serving bowl. Pour the dressing over the mixture and toss again. Sprinkle with chili powder, if using.

Winter Cauliflower and Broccoli Salad

SERVES 6 TO 8

We have served this salad at our café in the depth of winter when some of our customers want something more substantial than a simple lettuce salad. A sandwich and an order of Winter Cauliflower and Broccoli Salad on the side makes a hearty lunch. The tarragon and Italian parsley add lightness to the mayonnaise-sour cream dressing.

1 small head cauliflower, cut into small florets
1 medium bunch broccoli, cut into small florets
6 cherry tomatoes, seeded and cut into thin strips
2 Tbsp. (30 mL) mayonnaise

2 Tbsp. (30 mL) sour cream
1 Tbsp. (15 mL) Dijon mustard
kosher salt and freshly ground black pepper
1 tsp. (5 mL) finely chopped tarragon
1 small handful Italian parsley, roughly chopped

Steam the cauliflower for about 5 minutes, or until the florets are cooked through but still tender crisp. Run under cold water to stop the cooking process and drain.

Do the same with the broccoli, steaming for approximately 2 to 3 minutes before running under cold water.

Put the cooled and drained vegetables in a serving bowl with the tomato strips.

In a separate bowl, combine the mayonnaise, sour cream, and mustard. Season with salt and pepper.

Toss the dressing in with the vegetables and tarragon. Garnish with parsley and serve.

COOK'S TIP

Reduced-fat mayonnaise and sour cream work well in this recipe.

Boston Lettuce with Walnuts, Apple and Gruyère in a Citrus-Mint Vinaigrette

SERVES 4

Even though there are walnuts, apple, and Gruyère in this salad, the delicate Boston lettuce and citrus vinaigrette make it a light refreshing dish. It's important to dress it very lightly as the fragile leaves of the lettuce will wilt under a surplus of vinaigrette. If I'm using it to accompany a cheese course or a main course that has cheese as an ingredient, I make it without the Gruyère.

⅓ cup (80 mL) coarsely chopped walnuts
3 generous Tbsp. (45 mL) freshly squeezed lemon juice
½ tsp. (2.5 mL) kosher salt
2 Tbsp. (30 mL) extra-virgin olive oil
1 heaping tsp. (5 mL) organic mixed citrus zest
large pinch freshly ground black pepper
2 Tbsp. (30 mL) loosely packed julienned mint

½ Granny Smith apple, peeled, cored and cut into 1½- × ¼-inch (3.8-cm × 6-mm) batons or ½ unpeeled apple, cored and cut in ⅛-inch (3-mm) slices
1 to 3 heads Boston lettuce, depending on size, or enough for 4 people, cleaned
1½ oz. (42 g) Gruyère, cut in 1¼- × ⅛-inch (3-cm × 0.3-cm) matchsticks

Preheat the oven to 350°F (175°C), and lightly toast the walnut pieces on a baking sheet for about 4 minutes. Cool and reserve.

In a small bowl, whisk together the lemon juice and salt. Let sit for 5 minutes before whisking in the olive oil, zest, pepper, and mint.

In a larger bowl, gently but thoroughly toss the lettuce and apple batons with the vinaigrette. Plate and top each serving with walnuts and Gruyère matchsticks.

COOK'S TIP

If preparing ahead, submerge the pieces of apple in water with several teaspoons of freshly squeezed lemon juice for up to 30 minutes. This prevents the apples from turning brown. Just drain and pat dry when ready to add to the salad.

Flax Bread with Honey and Oats p. 24

Summer Radish, Cucumber and Italian Parsley Salad

SERVES 6 TO 8

By the time summer rolls around, I'm ready for light, crisp tastes that can be prepared with a minimum of fuss. This salad fits the bill. Serve it as an appetizer, with your favourite sandwich, to accompany a chicken burger, or as a side to barbecued chicken or fish.

1 English cucumber
10 to 12 radishes
½ bunch fresh Italian parsley, large stalks
   removed, about 3 loose cups (720 mL)
3 Tbsp. (45 mL) minced fresh chives
¾ cup (180 mL) coarsely crumbled feta

½ tsp. (2.5 mL) granulated sugar
½ tsp. (2.5 mL) kosher salt
1½ Tbsp. (22.5 mL) white wine vinegar
1 Tbsp. (15 mL) extra-virgin olive oil
freshly ground black pepper

Peel the cucumber, cut in half lengthwise, and scrape out the seeds with a teaspoon. Cut the flesh into ¼- to ½-inch (6-mm to 1.2-cm) cubes and place in a serving bowl.

Wash and thinly slice the radishes and add to the cucumber along with the parsley, chives, and ½ cup (120 mL) feta.

In a small bowl, stir the sugar and salt into the vinegar and let sit for 5 minutes. Whisk in the oil and the pepper. Taste and adjust seasoning—it should be light in taste with a slightly pronounced vinegary tang.

Toss the vinaigrette into the salad, top with the remaining feta, and serve immediately.

Arugula, Fig and Chèvre Salad with Red Wine Vinaigrette

SERVES 4

I had a salad very much like this one at Changa, a great restaurant in Istanbul. The chef had a few more ingredients in his salad, including capers and onions as well as a very strong vinaigrette. What I loved, though, was the combination of arugula, fresh figs, and chèvre. Dress it up or down—either way it's a great salad to precede or follow roasted Cornish hen or duck.

3 Tbsp. (45 mL) golden raisins
3 Tbsp. (45 mL) pine nuts
2 tsp. (10 mL) balsamic vinegar
1½ tsp. (7.5 mL) red wine vinegar
½ tsp. (2.5 mL) kosher salt
1½ Tbsp. (22.5 mL) extra-virgin olive oil
freshly ground black pepper to taste

2 bunches arugula, 3 if using Israeli arugula
3 fresh figs, cut into quarters
4 oz. (113 g) soft chèvre cut into 4 slices, then broken into 1-inch (2.5-cm) pieces
2 to 3 Tbsp. (30 to 45 mL) pomegranate seeds, optional

Preheat the oven to 375°F (190°C).

Plump the raisins by submerging them in hot water for 5 to 10 minutes. Drain and reserve.

Toast the pine nuts in the oven for about 4 minutes or until lightly golden. (They tend to burn, so keep an eye on them.) Set aside.

In a small bowl, whisk the vinegars together with the salt. Let sit for 5 minutes before whisking in the olive oil. Season with pepper.

Put the arugula and figs into a serving bowl and gently toss with vinaigrette. Sprinkle on the raisins, pine nuts, and, if using, the pomegranate seeds, and gently toss again. Top with the chèvre.

Alternatively, toss only the arugula with the vinaigrette. Divide among 4 plates, sprinkle with raisins, pine nuts and pomegranate seeds and tuck the pieces of fig and chèvre among the arugula leaves.

COOK'S TIP

All pine trees have nuts but most are too small to harvest. Pinyon Pines, which grow in the southwestern USA, and Stone Pines from Italy produce most of the nuts seen on grocery store shelves. Pine nuts turn rancid very quickly. Keep them in a cold room or in the refrigerator or freezer until ready to use.

Cranberry Pecan Wild Rice Salad

SERVES 4 TO 6

Wild rice and cranberries, so quintessentially Canadian, just belong together. And with a few orange segments in the salad and orange zest in the vinaigrette to complement the berries, you have a happy combination. Once you put the rice on to cook, it takes only 20 minutes of work to get this to the table. It's best served slightly warmer than room temperature and is lovely as part of a summer or autumn buffet. In the winter, I serve it with warm roast duck.

3 cups (720 mL) water
1 cup (240 mL) wild rice
½ cup (120 mL) dried cranberries
¼ to ½ cup (60 to 120 mL) roughly chopped
   pecan halves, toasted at 375°F (190°C) for
   4 minutes
5 green onions, whites and light green only,
   finely chopped

1 orange, peeled and segmented without pith
   (see Cook's Tip 1, page 174)
VINAIGRETTE
1 Tbsp. (15 mL) canola oil
2 Tbsp. (30 mL) freshly squeezed lemon juice
1 tsp. (5 mL) organic orange zest
kosher salt and freshly ground black pepper

Bring the water to a boil in a small saucepan. Stir in the rice and return to a boil. Reduce heat and simmer, covered, for about 45 to 50 minutes or until cooked. Remove from heat, drain off any excess water, fluff, and let cool slightly.

Cut the orange segments into ½-inch (1.2-cm) pieces. Once the rice is at room temperature or slightly warmer, add the cranberries, pecans, green onions, and orange pieces.

In a separate bowl, mix the oil, lemon juice, zest, salt, and pepper. Pour over the rice mixture and toss.

The long brown needles of wild rice are the seeds of a North American wild grass. Wild rice isn't related to the other rice we eat. Nutty in flavour, it's unmilled, with a tough outer layer; consequently, it can take up to 50 minutes to cook.

Israeli Couscous Salad with Spring Pea Mix

SERVES 6

You may have to search a little harder for Israeli couscous. It is larger than the more common North African couscous, but you'll be happy once you find it—its texture is quite different. Now there would be nothing wrong with making this salad with the North African cousin but it will be a completely different experience. In my kitchen I substitute orzo if I can't find Israeli couscous because the texture is similar and the cooking method the same.

1 cup (240 mL) uncooked Israeli couscous
1 tsp. (5 mL) kosher salt
½ cup (120 mL) fresh sugar snap peas
½ cup (120 mL) fresh snow peas
½ cup (120 mL) fresh or frozen green peas
1 Tbsp. (15 mL) safflower oil

1 Tbsp. (15 mL) freshly squeezed lemon juice
2 tsp. (10 mL) grated lemon zest
1 Tbsp. (15 mL) minced chives
4 Tbsp. (60 mL) chopped fresh mint
freshly ground black pepper

Bring a pot of water to a rolling boil. Add ½ tsp. (2.5 mL) of the salt and the Israeli couscous, and cook for about 8 minutes or until the couscous is tender. Drain, rinse with cold water, and let drain again for about 15 to 20 minutes.

Steam the sugar snap peas for 3 to 4 minutes until just done. Run under cold water until cool so that the peas retain their colour. Steam the snow peas for 1 minute while boiling the green peas. (Frozen peas will take 2 to 4 minutes while fresh peas will be ready in about 4 to 6 minutes.) Run both under cold water as soon as they are cooked. Drain all the peas and allow to dry.

Slice the snow peas diagonally into 3 or 4 pieces each.

Spoon the couscous into a serving bowl and toss with the peas. Sprinkle with the oil and lemon juice and toss to thoroughly coat the grains. Taste and add more oil or lemon juice if needed. Gently mix in the zest, chives, mint, remaining ½ tsp. (2.5 mL) salt, and pepper.

Serve at room temperature.

Brussels Sprouts and Bacon Salad
p. 112

Warm Roasted Sweet Potato
and Pear Salad

Warm Roasted Sweet Potato and Pear Salad

SERVES 4

The combination of warm, roasted sweet potatoes and crisp fresh pear is heavenly. With a little Pont L'Eveque or Camembert and a baguette it could be lunch. I also like it as a side dish to the Stuffed Pork Chops with Pomegranate Maple Glaze (see page 143) or as an accompaniment to roast turkey. Apple and Orange Walnut Cake (see page 184) would be a fitting ending.

2 medium sweet potatoes, about 1¾ lbs. (800 g)
2 Tbsp. (30 mL) olive oil
¼ heaping tsp. (1.2 mL) ground cinnamon
¼ heaping tsp. (1.2 mL) ground cumin
¼ tsp. (1.2 mL) cayenne pepper
large pinch kosher salt
¼ cup (60 mL) vegetable oil

2 to 3 large shallots, peeled and thinly sliced
1 to 2 crisp eating pears

VINAIGRETTE
1 Tbsp. (15 mL) freshly squeezed lemon juice
1 Tbsp. (15 mL) freshly squeezed orange juice
1½ Tbsp. (22.5 mL) extra-virgin olive oil
2 Tbsp. (30 mL) minced fresh basil
kosher salt and freshly ground black pepper

Preheat the oven to 400°F (200°C).

Peel the sweet potatoes and cut into 1-inch (2.5-cm) cubes. Toss with 2 Tbsp. (30 mL) olive oil, cinnamon, cumin, cayenne, and salt. Roast for 25 to 30 minutes, turning once or twice until cooked through and golden brown.

While the potatoes are roasting, heat the vegetable oil in a shallow pot. Add the sliced shallots in batches and fry, stirring, until they are dark golden and crispy. Drain and reserve. Spoon the warm potatoes into a serving bowl. Core and cut the pears into ⅛-inch (3-mm) slices and add to the sweet potatoes.

In a small bowl, stir together the lemon and orange juice. Whisk in the olive oil and then the basil. Season with salt and pepper.

Gently toss the vinaigrette into the sweet potatoes and pears and sprinkle with the crispy shallots.

Serve while the sweet potatoes are still warm.

Enza's Tomatoes Stuffed with Shrimp, Tuna or Egg

SERVES 6

Years ago, when our children were toddlers, we rented a house near Siena, Italy, with my parents. After the transatlantic flight and three-hour drive to the villa, we were greeted by Enza, the cook, who had prepared tomatoes stuffed with tuna as part of our lunch. Looking out over the hills of Tuscany from our new terrace, we were convinced that life couldn't get any better. Here are three variations on Enza's stuffed tomatoes. Try making all three variations with different coloured tomatoes and serve them on a lettuce-covered platter, accompanied by Flax Bread with Honey and Oats (see page 24) or Cheddar Roll Cluster (see page 21).

24 jumbo shrimp, cleaned
OR
8 extra-large hard-boiled eggs, peeled and
 chopped
6 large or 12 medium ripe tomatoes
MAYONNAISE DRESSING FOR 24 SHRIMP
 (to fill 6 large or 12 medium tomatoes)
¼ cup (60 mL) homemade or good quality
 store-bought mayonnaise
2 tsp. (10 mL) freshly squeezed lemon juice
2 tsp. (10 mL) minced fresh chives
kosher salt and freshly ground white pepper

VINAIGRETTE FOR 24 SHRIMP
 (to fill 6 large or 12 medium tomatoes)
1 tsp. (15 mL) Dijon mustard
1½ tsp. (7.5 mL) white wine vinegar
1 tsp. (5 mL) freshly squeezed lemon juice
¼ cup (90 mL) extra-virgin olive oil
1 Tbsp. (15 mL) small capers
kosher salt and freshly ground white pepper
DRESSING FOR 8 EGGS
 (to fill 6 large or 12 small tomatoes)
8 Tbsp. (120 mL) homemade or good quality,
 store-bought mayonnaise
3 Tbsp. (45 mL) minced fresh dill
kosher salt and freshly ground black pepper

pitted black olives, dill sprigs, chiffonade of
 fresh basil and Boston lettuce for garnish

FOR THE SHRIMP

To steam the shrimp, wrap 6 shrimp in parchment paper, folding the ends over to make a package. Continue with the rest of the shrimp—6 to a packet. Place on a steamer over boiling water. Cover and steam until just cooked through. The shrimp will take about 5 to 6 minutes, depending on size. Remove from the parchment paper while still warm—a messy job. Discard the juices and let shrimp cool.

FOR THE SHRIMP WITH MAYONNAISE

Spoon the mayonnaise into a bowl large enough to hold the shrimp. Add the lemon juice and chives, and mix. Season with salt and pepper and toss in the shrimp.

FOR THE TUNA

Enza's version is to use tuna instead of shrimp. You can use canned tuna in olive oil, adjusting the mayonnaise accordingly.

FOR THE SHRIMP WITH VINAIGRETTE

Spoon the mustard into a small bowl. Whisk in the white wine vinegar and the lemon juice. Continue whisking while slowly dribbling in the oil until the mixture emulsifies. Add the capers, and salt and pepper to taste. Pour half the vinaigrette with most of the capers over the shrimp and toss. Add more vinaigrette if needed. Reserve any extra vinaigrette to toss over lettuce or to drizzle over grilled white fish.

FOR THE EGG SALAD

Spoon the mayonnaise into a bowl large enough to contain the chopped hard-boiled eggs (see Cook's Tip). Add the minced dill and toss the eggs in the dressing. Season with salt and pepper. Extra egg salad can be kept refrigerated for 2 days.

ASSEMBLY

Core the tomatoes with a melon baller. Sprinkle with salt and place cut-side down on paper towels to drain for 20 minutes. Pat the insides of the tomatoes dry with paper towel and fill, heaping generously with any of the three mixtures. Top each egg-stuffed tomato with a sprig of dill and an olive. Top the shrimp-stuffed tomatoes with basil and serve on a bed of lettuce.

COOK'S TIPS

1. Prepare hard-boiled eggs the way restaurant kitchens do: rub the peeled, whole eggs through the large-hole side of a grater. (See Cook's Tip page 124 for boiling eggs.)

2. When cutting basil, roll the leaves up like a jellyroll for easy cutting. Cut basil at the last moment as the cutting can bruise and darken the leaves.

Brussels Sprouts and Bacon Salad with French Vinaigrette

SERVES 4 TO 6

If you aren't a fan of cooked sprouts, and even if you are, you'll find their taste very different when tossed in vinaigrette and served at room temperature. This salad (photo page 108) has all the ingredients that go well with a cabbage family member—bacon, mustard, lemon, and oil—but it's a lighter, fresher alternative to the hot version. I serve it with cold meats for lunch, as an appetizer, or with turkey, wild fowl, or venison. The trick to getting it just right is adding thickly-cut bacon—¼ inch (6 mm) is optimum.

three ¼-inch-thick (6-mm) slices bacon, cut in ¼-inch (6-mm) cubes
2 Tbsp. (30 mL) finely minced shallots
30 Brussels sprouts, halved and cut in ⅛-inch (3-mm) slices, about 7 cups (1.7 L) when sliced
½ tsp. (2.5 mL) poppy seeds

FRENCH VINAIGRETTE
1 tsp. (5 mL) Dijon mustard
1 Tbsp. (15 mL) freshly squeezed lemon juice
¼ tsp. (1.2 mL) kosher salt
1 tsp. (5 mL) red wine vinegar
2 Tbsp. (30 mL) extra-virgin olive oil

In a medium frying pan, sauté the bacon over medium heat for about 10 minutes or until it has rendered its fat and is quite crisp and a rosy brown. Drain and set aside.

Using some of the bacon fat, sauté the shallots for about 1½ to 2 minutes over medium heat until soft and pale golden. Drain and set aside.

Bring a large saucepan of lightly salted water to a boil and blanch the Brussels sprouts for about 1 minute. They will turn a vibrant green. Pour into a colander and run under cold water until cool to stop the cooking process. Drain and pat dry with paper towels.

In a small bowl, combine the mustard, lemon juice, salt, vinegar, and olive oil. Let rest for 5 minutes before whisking in the reserved shallots.

In a serving bowl, gently mix together the Brussels sprouts and bacon. Pour in the dressing and toss. Sprinkle with poppy seeds and serve at room temperature, or slightly warmer.

Vinaigrette, a simple mixture of oil and vinegar, is perhaps the most commonly used salad dressing. The name comes from the French vin aigre, meaning "sharp or sour wine." Although it only became popular in the West around 1880, the Babylonians used oil and vinegar to dress greens over 2000 years ago.

Sandwiches

Prosciutto, Basil and Bocconcini Panini with Sun-Dried Tomato Pesto   116

Grilled Mediterranean Eggplant, Ham and Feta   117

ACE Grilled Blue Cheese, Parmigiano Reggiano and Bresaola on Raisin Walnut   118

Chicken Club for a Crowd   119

Luke's Spicy Sausage with Caramelized Onions on Ficelle   120

Roasted Portobello with Herbed Cheeses on Baguette   122

Rosalind's Medium-Rare Roast Beef with Avocado and Tomato Mayo
on Multigrain   123

"Really, Really Nice Egg Sandwich" on Flax Bread   124

Italian Flag Tramezzino on Calabrese   127

Summer Garden Tuna on Whole Wheat   129

Shaved Parmigiano Reggiano with Tomatoes and Tapenade on Ficelle   130

Pear and Brie on Raisin Walnut   133

Gingered Limeade   134

"I like the philosophy of the sandwich, as it were. It typifies my attitude to life, really. It is all there, it's fun, it looks good, and you don't have to wash up afterwards."

—Molly Parkin

Prosciutto, Basil and Bocconcini Panini with Sun-Dried Tomato Pesto

MAKES 2 SANDWICHES

We have made a sandwich similar to this for years at the café. It's at its best grilled, but is also enjoyable au naturel. For a vegetarian option, add a touch more Sun-Dried Tomato Pesto and omit the meat. If time is of the essence, buy the pesto at your local grocery store.

4 tsp. (20 mL) Sun-Dried Tomato Pesto (see page 76) or good quality store-bought sun-dried tomato pesto
4 slices white or Calabrese bread or 2 large rolls sliced horizontally
4 to 6 slices prosciutto

2 bocconcini, roughly 2 inches (5 cm) in diameter
coarsely ground black pepper
fresh basil leaves
extra-virgin olive oil to brush bread

Spread 2 tsp. (10 mL) of the Sun-Dried Tomato Pesto on one side of 2 slices of bread or on the bottom part of the rolls. Cover the pesto-spread slices with prosciutto.

Cut the bocconcini into ¼-inch (6-mm) thick slices and place over the prosciutto. Top the cheese with a generous grind of black pepper and cover with basil leaves. Finish the sandwiches with the remaining slices of bread or top of the rolls.

Brush both sides of the sandwich with olive oil and grill until the cheese has melted and the bread is golden.

Bocconcini, small balls of fresh mozzarella, means "mouthful" in Italian — meant not as a reference to its size but to the enjoyable taste. Consequently, the word "bocconcini" is sometimes used to describe Italian dishes that don't contain the cheese.

Grilled Mediterranean Eggplant, Ham and Feta

MAKES 2 SANDWICHES

Grilled eggplant and feta are an exquisite combination. Like most grilled cheese sandwiches, this one can be made without the meat. If this is the way you want to go, add a few chopped black olives in its stead.

4 slices white or Calabrese bread or 2 large
  rolls sliced horizontally
2 slices roasted or grilled eggplant (see
  page 138)
4 thin slices Black Forest or Tuscan smoked
  ham

6 to 8 cherry tomatoes, halved
3 to 4 Tbsp. (45 to 60 mL) crumbled feta
  cheese
2 small handfuls arugula
extra-virgin olive oil to brush bread

Layer 2 slices of bread or the bottom part of the rolls with roasted eggplant, ham, tomatoes, feta, and arugula. Top each with another slice of bread or roll top.

Brush both sides of each sandwich with olive oil and grill until the cheese has melted and the bread is golden.

Cut in half and serve while still warm.

Arab traders brought eggplant to Spain and North Africa in the Middle Ages. It became popular in Italy in the 15th century. Although we think of eggplant as a vegetable, it is classified as a berry.

ACE Grilled Blue Cheese, Parmigiano Reggiano and Bresaola on Raisin Walnut

MAKES 2 SANDWICHES

Bresaola, an Italian salted and air-dried beef fillet, is often served on its own, sliced very thinly and drizzled with oil and lemon juice. But because of its unique texture and rich, smoky taste, it pairs well with blue cheese. A dense artisan raisin walnut bread and Spiced Pear Ketchup (see page 77) are essential to this recipe.

4 to 6 slices bresaola (air-dried beef)
4 slices artisan raisin walnut or white bread
1½ oz. (42 g) mild blue cheese, crumbled
½ oz. (14 g) freshly grated Parmigiano Reggiano

2 to 3 tsp. (10 to 15 mL) unsalted butter, softened
¼ cup (60 mL) Spiced Pear Ketchup (see page 77)

Layer the bresaola on two slices of bread. Top each with blue cheese and Parmigiano Reggiano and cover with the other two slices of bread.

Butter the outsides of each sandwich. Fry both sides in a warm, nonstick pan until the bread is golden and the cheese is melted.

Cut in four triangles while still warm and dip each mouthful in the Spiced Pear Ketchup.

Chicken Club for a Crowd

MAKES 6 (4-INCH/10-CM) SANDWICHES

Just a trip to the store and all the components for this tasty mega sandwich will be in your kitchen: a roasted chicken, bottled red peppers, pesto, mayonnaise, fontina cheese, and a few herbs. All you will have to do is fry the bacon and layer your ingredients into a top-quality artisan baguette. You'll find this is great picnic food. Wrap the whole sandwich in tin foil or waxed paper (plastic wrap will soften the bread's crust) and cut it into pieces on site. I have made up a couple for a Super Bowl party and served them with the Tomato, Ginger and Orange Soup with Mini Croutons (see page 81), the Winter Cauliflower and Broccoli Salad (see page 99), and the Gingered Fennel and Apple Slaw with Buttermilk Dressing (see page 97).

2 roasted single chicken breasts
6 to 8 slices bacon
½ cup (120 mL) mayonnaise
3 to 4 Tbsp. (45 to 60 mL) Tuscan Pesto (see page 75) or good quality, store-bought pesto
1 baguette

6 to 8 leaves Boston lettuce
1 small jar roasted red peppers, drained and patted dry
3 to 4 oz. (85 to 113 g) sliced fontina cheese
kosher salt and freshly ground black pepper

Slice the chicken into ¼-inch (6-mm) slices and set aside. Fry the bacon and drain on a paper towel. Mix the mayonnaise and pesto together in a small bowl.

Cut the baguette horizontally so that you have a top and bottom half. Spread the bottom half with a small amount of the pesto mayonnaise and layer the lettuce, chicken, bacon, cheese, and peppers. Season with salt and pepper and top with remaining baguette half. Cut into 6 pieces to serve.

COOK'S TIP

The extra pesto mayonnaise and chicken will keep in the refrigerator for up to 3 days, the peppers for 1 week.

Luke's Spicy Sausage with Caramelized Onions on Ficelle

MAKES 4 (5-INCH / 12.5-CM) SANDWICHES

Our son, Luke, and his teenage friends were crazy about this combination of spicy sausage and golden brown onions. We have since retired it from the menu at the café but I'm still making it at home. The little bit of Dijon mustard and the drizzle of basil oil take this warm sandwich to another level. A ficelle (the French word for string or twine), is a long, thin bread only 1½ to 2 inches (3.8 to 5 cm) in diameter. Think of it as a very skinny baguette.

2 Tbsp. (30 mL) olive oil
3 to 4 medium cooking onions, sliced
½ tsp. (2.5 mL) granulated sugar
4 thin dry-cured hot chorizo or other dry-cured spicy sausages or 2 larger "fatter" sausages

1 ficelle, about 20 inches (50 cm) long
2 tsp. (10 mL) Dijon mustard
2 to 4 tsp. (10 to 20 mL) Basil Oil (see opposite page)

Preheat the oven to 400°F (200°C).

Heat the olive oil in a sauté pan over medium heat and add the onions. Sauté for 20 minutes on medium-low heat, stirring occasionally until the onions are browned. Add the sugar and sauté 5 minutes more or until onions are caramelized and dark brown in colour; set aside.

Meanwhile, in a lightly oiled medium frying pan, fry the sausages over medium heat until cooked through. Remove sausages from the pan and let rest a few minutes, and, if large, slice them in half lengthwise.

Cut open from the top, but not through, the ficelle and spread 1 to 2 tsp. (5 to 10 mL) Dijon mustard on one half of the bread. Cover with a layer of caramelized onions and a layer of sausage and hold closed with a toothpick. Place in the hot oven for 2 minutes to warm the sandwich through.

Remove the warmed ficelle from oven and cut in quarters. Drizzle Basil Oil into each sandwich quarter before serving.

COOK'S TIP

Check the label when buying Dijon mustard. Many well-known brands contain sulfates. To be sure you are getting just mustard seeds and other natural ingredients, buy organic.

Basil Oil

MAKES ½ TO ⅔ CUP (120 TO 160 mL)

This recipe makes more oil than needed for the sandwiches but it can be kept in the refrigerator for up to a week and makes a great dip or topping for fish.

1 cup (240 mL) lightly packed, washed
  basil leaves
1 medium garlic clove, roughly chopped
½ cup (120 mL) extra-virgin olive oil

Place basil, garlic, and oil in a blender. Blend until well combined. Store in a jar, tightly covered, or in a squeeze bottle in the refrigerator.

"A man taking basil from a woman will love her always."

—Sir Thomas Moore

Roasted Portobello with Herbed Cheeses on Baguette

MAKES 6 (4-INCH / 10-CM) SANDWICHES

Michelle Heywood, our Quality and Customer Service Manager, created this appealing combination of roasted mushrooms and chèvre. It has been on our menu for two years and is still our most popular sandwich. The cooked mushrooms and cheese mixture will last a few days in the refrigerator. Bring them to room temperature before making your sandwich.

3 Portobello mushrooms
3 Tbsp. (45 mL) olive oil + 1½ tsp. (7.5 mL) for cheese mixture
kosher salt and freshly ground black pepper
½ cup (120 mL) soft chèvre, at room temperature
2 Tbsp. + 2 tsp. (40 mL) grated Asiago cheese

1 medium garlic clove, finely minced
2 Tbsp. (30 mL) drained and minced oil-packed sun-dried tomatoes
1½ tsp. (7.5 mL) finely chopped fresh basil
1 tsp. (5 mL) finely chopped fresh oregano
1 baguette
4 to 6 leaves Boston lettuce

Preheat the oven to 400°F (200°C).

Carefully remove the stems from the Portobello mushrooms. Drizzle the inside of each mushroom cap with 1 Tbsp. (15 mL) olive oil and season with salt and pepper. Place mushroom caps, with oil-drizzled inside facing up, on a baking tray and roast for 12 to 15 minutes or until caps are slightly wrinkled. Remove from oven, cool, and cut into thin ⅛-inch (3-mm) strips.

Combine the chèvre, Asiago, garlic, sun-dried tomatoes, basil, oregano, and the remaining 1½ tsp. (7.5 mL) olive oil in a medium bowl; mash together with a fork. Cover and refrigerate until ready to use.

Cut open the baguette along the side, three-quarters of the way through. Spread the bottom half with the cheese mix and cover with a layer of mushroom slices. Arrange the lettuce on top of the mushrooms and close the baguette. Cut into 6 pieces and serve.

Fresh oregano leaves can be chewed to deaden toothache or brewed into tea to alleviate indigestion. Oregano oil, available at health food stores, is used to treat sore throats and coughs.

Rosalind's Medium-Rare Roast Beef with Avocado and Tomato Mayo on Multigrain

MAKES 2 SANDWICHES

Rosalind Whelan, ACE Bakery's Administration Manager, came up with the idea for this delicious sandwich, which quickly made its way onto the café menu. The trick here is to cover the entire bread slice with a layer of thinly sliced medium-rare roast beef and avocado. A fairly dense multigrain bread is also a must. The creaminess of the avocado contrasted with the textured grain bread makes for a beautiful marriage. Don't be tempted to add slices of whole tomatoes—too much tomato will overpower this sandwich.

1 medium tomato, seeded and finely minced
2 Tbsp. (30 mL) mayonnaise
1½ tsp. (7.5 mL) Dijon mustard
2 tsp. (10 mL) minced fresh chives
4 slices multigrain bread

4 to 6 thin slices medium-rare roast beef
½ avocado, peeled, pitted, and thinly sliced
kosher salt and freshly ground black pepper
2 to 4 leaves Boston lettuce (optional)

In a small bowl, mix together the tomato, mayonnaise, mustard, and chives. Spread the mayonnaise mixture on one side of 2 slices of bread.

Layer the roast beef over each bread slice, followed by the avocado slices. Season with salt and pepper and top with lettuce, if using, and the remaining bread slices.

Cut each sandwich in half on the diagonal and serve.

"Really, Really Nice Egg Sandwich" on Flax Bread

MAKES 2 VERY GENEROUS SANDWICHES

When my husband, Martin, first tasted this sandwich, he announced that it was a "really, really nice egg sandwich." The name has stuck. Yogurt takes the place of the usual mayonnaise, making it lighter but giving it a bit of a tang. The asparagus add a springtime touch. This sandwich looks very appealing when served open-faced.

3 eggs, hard boiled (see Cook's Tip)
6 to 8 asparagus stalks
3 Tbsp. (45 mL) 2% or 4% yogurt
heaping ¼ tsp. (1.2 mL) Dijon mustard
2 tsp. (10 mL) minced fresh chives
generous ¼ tsp. (1.2 mL) freshly squeezed
   lemon juice

heaping ¼ tsp. (1.2 mL) kosher salt
⅛ tsp. freshly ground white pepper
2 to 4 leaves Boston lettuce
2 to 4 slices Flax Bread with Honey and Oats
   (see page 24) or multigrain bread
1 large tomato, sliced
freshly ground black pepper

Hard-boil the eggs (see Cook's Tip). While the eggs are cooking, steam the asparagus until cooked through. Shock in cold water to retain the colour, drain, and pat dry.

In a medium bowl, whisk together the yogurt, mustard, chives, lemon juice, kosher salt, and white pepper.

Peel and coarsely grate the hard-boiled eggs (use the large holes of a grater) into the yogurt-mustard dressing bowl. Gently toss the dressing into the eggs. Taste and add more salt and pepper if needed.

Place the lettuce on the bread slices and top with tomato slices. Spoon on the egg salad and arrange the asparagus on top. Finish with a grind of black pepper and serve open-faced or top with another slice of bread.

COOK'S TIP

My favourite way to hard-boil eggs is to start them in cold water. Cover the pot and bring to a boil for 30 seconds. Remove from the heat and let the eggs rest, covered in the hot water, for 15 minutes. Plunge immediately into cold water and leave to cool to prevent a dark ring from forming around the yolks.

Gingered Limeade p. 134

Italian Flag Tramezzino on Calabrese

MAKES 2 SANDWICHES

Tomatoes, fontina, and arugula, all found in plenitude in the Italian kitchen, are the basis of this flavourful tramezzino—an Italian word for sandwich. Coincidentally they also represent the colours of the Italian flag (red, white, and green). Michelle Heywood, from ACE and a fan of Italian food, suggested this winning combination.

2 to 3 tsp. (10 to 15 mL) roasted garlic purée (see method page 68)

4 slices Calabrese or country bread

2 roasted and peeled red bell peppers (see method page 71) at room temperature or bottled red peppers, rinsed, patted dry, and cut into strips

8 thin slices Italian fontina cheese

1 small handful fresh arugula, rinsed and dried

2 tsp. Parsley Chive Purée (see page 128)

Spread a thin layer of roasted garlic purée on 2 slices of bread. Arrange a layer of red pepper strips over the garlic spread and top with fontina cheese and arugula. Spread a thin layer of Parsley Chive Purée on the remaining slices of bread and place over the arugula to form a sandwich.

Calabrese was first made in the province of Calabria in southern Italy. It is a natural for crostinis and sandwiches because of its even crumb. At ACE we add a touch of rye and corn flour to the mix and dust the top with cornmeal. My recipe for Calabrese is in The ACE Bakery Cookbook: Recipes for and with Bread.

Parsley Chive Purée

MAKES ⅔ CUP (160 mL)

This recipe makes a large quantity of purée, but the excess is unavoidable: blending a smaller amount just doesn't work very well. You can keep the extra purée in the refrigerator for up to two weeks. When ready to use, just return it to room temperature and use as a dip or a drizzle over fish or vegetables.

¼ cup minced fresh chives
¾ cup packed fresh Italian parsley, large stems
   removed
½ cup (120 mL) extra-virgin olive oil

Purée the chives, parsley, and oil in a blender and store in a clean jar or squeeze bottle in the refrigerator.

COOK'S TIP
Finely chopped parsley will keep fresh in the refrigerator for up to 2 days if blotted with paper towels, wrapped in fresh paper towel, and then placed in a plastic bag.

Summer Garden Tuna on Whole Wheat

MAKES 3 SANDWICHES

Tarragon, a popular herb in French cooking, marries well with fish and vegetables. It is "assertive" (or intensely flavoured), so use it judiciously. You'll have to do a little chopping, but you'll be happy with the final result.

2 cans (170 g) flaked white tuna, drained
1 medium carrot, peeled and finely chopped
1 celery stalk, about 8 inches (20 cm) long, finely chopped
2 radishes, thinly sliced and julienned
1 tsp. (5 mL) finely minced fresh tarragon

4 to 5 Tbsp. (60 to 75 mL) mayonnaise
kosher salt and freshly ground black pepper
1 large squeeze lemon juice
4 to 6 leaves Boston lettuce
6 slices whole wheat, Calabrese, or white bread

Flake the tuna in a medium bowl and add the carrot, celery, radishes, tarragon, and mayonnaise. Mix well, adding more mayonnaise if desired and stir in salt, pepper, and lemon juice. Adjust the seasoning to taste and spread the mixture on one side of each of the bread slices. Top tuna with the lettuce and remaining bread slices. Cut each sandwich into quarters and serve.

Shaved Parmigiano Reggiano with Tomatoes and Tapenade on Ficelle

MAKES 2 (10-INCH/25-CM) SANDWICHES

Although Parmigiano Reggiano is wonderful grated over pasta, it is equally good eaten on its own or in a sandwich. The only caveat is that you must be prepared to buy Parmigiano Reggiano from Italy and not an inferior type of cheese. This sandwich has been a part of the summer menu at our Fresh Bread Store and Café for many years. The tomatoes and basil peek out of the top, making for a sandwich that is as pretty as it is delicious.

1 ficelle (see introduction, page 120,
   for definition)
2 Tbsp. (30 mL) tapenade or olive paste
1 oz. (30 g) shaved Parmigiano Reggiano
4 to 5 slices tomato, cut in half
8 to 10 fresh basil leaves
coarsely ground black pepper

Using a bread knife, slice open the ficelle from the top, three-quarters of the way through the bread.

Spread the tapenade along one side of the bread.

Place the shaved Parmigiano Reggiano evenly along the ficelle.

Cover with an overlapping layer of tomato slices so that the rounded ends are peeking out of the ficelle.

Add basil leaves overtop the tomatoes and near the edge, to peek out of the bread. Finish with a generous grind of black pepper, press the two sides of bread together, cut in half, and serve.

COOK'S TIP

If you don't have a Swedish cheese planer or an extremely sharp knife, use a vegetable peeler to "shave" Parmigiano Reggiano.

Pear and Brie on Raisin Walnut

MAKES 2 SANDWICHES

Every cookbook needs a recipe that can be ready in five minutes, and this is it. The one prerequisite is that you use a dense, artisan-style raisin walnut bread—although a full bodied multigrain can be substituted in a pinch. The bread must have enough substance to counter the sweet and pungent filling. Encasing the brie between two layers of pear cuts the richness of the cheese and adds a delicious crunchy texture to the sandwich. Mariola Keszycki, our Fresh Bread Store and Café Manager, came up with this decadent marriage of flavours.

1 to 2 tsp. (5 to 10 mL) honey mustard (optional)	1 Bosc or other crisp pear, cored and cut in ⅛-inch (3-mm) slices
4 slices or 2 large rolls artisan raisin walnut bread	5 oz. (140 g) brie, cut in ¼-inch (6-mm) slices
	1 large handful watercress, washed and dried

Spread a thin layer of honey mustard on one side of each of the bread slices (optional). Cover with pear slices, then slices of brie. Finish with another layer of pear, and a thin layer of watercress. Top with remaining bread slices, cut each sandwich in half, and serve.

Although we all know that raisins are simply dried grapes, golden and dark raisins are processed in different ways. Golden raisins are treated with sulphur dioxide and dried with artificial heat, while dark raisins are sundried for several weeks.

Gingered Limeade

MAKES ABOUT 6 CUPS (1.5 L)

Persian and Bearss are the type of limes most often found in supermarkets. Gourmet stores sometimes carry kaffir, key, or rangpur limes. All limes are more perishable than lemons and should be kept in a perforated plastic bag in the refrigerator. When you've had one glass too many of lemonade, give this a try (photo page 126).

4 cups (950 mL) water
½ cup (120 mL) granulated sugar
3 slices fresh ginger, ⅛-inch (3-mm) thick and
   1-inch (2.5-cm) in diameter
1⅓ cups lime juice (320 mL), about 5 large
   limes
2 cups (480 mL) ice cubes
washed strawberries, for garnish

In a medium saucepan, bring 1 cup (240 mL) water and all the sugar to a simmer, stirring occasionally to make sure the sugar doesn't burn. Once the sugar has dissolved, remove from heat, and add the ginger. Infuse for a half hour. By this time the syrup will have cooled to room temperature. Discard the ginger.

Pour the lime juice into a large pitcher and mix in 1 cup (240 mL) of the sugar syrup. Stir in the remaining water and the ice cubes. Add more sugar syrup if the limeade is too tart for your taste.

Pour into glasses and garnish each glass with one sliced strawberry.

COOK'S TIP

To get the most juice possible from a lime make sure it's at room temperature (a few seconds in a micro-wave will help). Before juicing, roll it around on a countertop to soften, applying pressure with the palm of your hand.

There are three main types of lime: Tahitian, Mexican, and Key limes, which vary in size, colour, flavour, and aroma. Despite being the smallest members of the citrus family, certain limes can have one and a half times as much acid as a lemon of the same weight. Though they are always picked "green," limes will become orange if left to ripen on the tree.

Dinner and Sides

Greek Lamb Charlotte with Lemon-Mint Hollandaise

SERVES 4 TO 6

This recipe, while long, is simple to make. A lot of the length has to do with describing the technique of creating the bread casing for the tantalizing lamb, eggplant, and tomato filling. Fresh oregano, mint, and toasted pine nuts all add to the scrumptious flavour. The Lemon-Mint Hollandaise is the finishing touch. The charlotte can be prepared ahead of time and popped in the oven about 1 hour before you sit down for dinner.

1 large eggplant, cut in ¼-inch (6-mm) slices (you will need 15 slices)

1 to 2 tsp. (5 to 10 mL) kosher salt + 1 tsp. (5 mL) kosher salt for the filling

1 Tbsp. (15 mL) good quality olive oil (for brushing eggplant)

4 Tbsp. (60 mL) good quality olive oil

½ cup (120 mL) chopped yellow cooking onion

2 Tbsp. (30 mL) finely minced garlic

1¾ lbs. (800 g) coarsely ground lamb

¼ tsp. (1.2 mL) freshly ground black pepper

1 Tbsp. (15 mL) finely chopped fresh oregano leaves

2 Tbsp. (30 mL) finely chopped fresh mint leaves

1 tsp. (5 mL) ground cinnamon

1 large egg

½ cup (120 mL) fresh breadcrumbs (see Cook's Tip, page 168)

¼ cup (60 mL) toasted pine nuts (see method, page 104)

sixteen to twenty ½-inch (1.2-cm) slices white bread (sandwich-loaf shaped, crusts removed)

½ to ⅔ cup (120 to 160 mL) melted unsalted butter

12 to 24 cherry tomatoes, stemmed and washed

LEMON-MINT HOLLANDAISE (SEE PAGE 140)

Preheat the oven to 400°F (200°C).

Place the eggplant slices on a paper towel and sprinkle both sides with 1 to 2 tsp. (5 to 10 mL) salt. Leave to drain for 30 minutes. Pat dry and lightly brush with 1 Tbsp. (15 mL) olive oil. (You may have some oil left over.) Bake for 10 minutes and let cool.

Reduce the oven temperature to 375°F (190°C).

Pour 2 Tbsp. (30 mL) olive oil into a sauté pan large enough to hold the onions, ground lamb, and herbs. Sauté the onions in the pan over medium-low heat for 4 to 5 minutes or until softened but not coloured.

Add the remaining 2 Tbsp. (30 mL) olive oil, if needed, and the garlic, and cook for another 30 seconds. Stir in the lamb and increase the heat to medium. Sauté until the lamb has almost cooked through. Mix in the 1 tsp. (5 mL) salt, pepper, oregano, mint, and cinnamon, and cook for another minute until all the lamb is brown.

Allow the lamb to cool to room temperature. Lightly whisk the egg and stir into the lamb. Add the breadcrumbs and pine nuts and stir to combine; set aside.

Brush 1 side of each piece of bread with melted butter. Cut enough slices of bread into triangles to line the bottom of an 8-cup (2-L) charlotte tin. The triangles should be placed overlapping and butter-side down to completely cover the bottom of the tin. Brush lightly with more melted butter. Cut the rest of the bread in half, horizontally, and line the sides of the pan, butter-side out. Again, slightly overlap the slices of bread. The bread should cover all of the sides and reach to the top of the pan. The extra bread will be used later in the recipe.

Fit a layer (not overlapping) of eggplant slices over the bottom layer of bread. Spread 1 cup (240 mL) lamb mixture over the eggplant. Press down on the lamb and add a second layer of eggplant and another generous cup (240 mL) of lamb, pressing down again. Follow with a single layer of tomatoes. Gently press down. Finish with the remaining lamb, pressing down as necessary to fit into the charlotte tin.

Overlap the rest of the bread, butter-side down, in a circle over the lamb and brush the top with more melted butter.

Bake for 30 to 40 minutes or until the interior is heated through. Check after 15 minutes to make sure the top is not over-browning. If it is, cover the charlotte with tin foil for the remaining 20 to 25 minutes of baking time. Insert a thin knife into the interior. The blade will be quite warm to the touch when the lamb is ready. Remove the charlotte from the oven and let rest for 15 minutes before turning it out onto a serving dish.

Cut into pie-shaped pieces and serve with Lemon-Mint Hollandaise (see page 140).

Metal charlotte tins look like angel food tins without the centre cone. A light-coloured metal charlotte tin will produce darker golden sides than a teflon-lined pan. It's hard to find a substitute although an 8 to 10 cup round soufflé dish can be used. It will take longer for the bread to turn golden and the lamb to heat through.

Lemon-Mint Hollandaise

MAKES 1 CUP (240 ML)

3 extra-large eggs
1 Tbsp. + 1 tsp. (20 mL) freshly squeezed
  lemon juice
1 Tbsp. (15 mL) water, at room temperature
pinch cayenne pepper
⅔ cup (160 mL) unsalted butter
¼ tsp. (1.2 mL) kosher salt
pinch freshly ground white pepper
2 Tbsp. (30 mL) minced fresh mint

Separate the eggs and reserve the whites for another use. Place the yolks in the top part of a double boiler. Whisk in 1 Tbsp. (15 mL) lemon juice, water, and the cayenne pepper.

Melt the butter in a small saucepan and skim off the foam that rises to the top.

Heat some water in the bottom of the double boiler and, when it comes to a simmer, place the eggs on top, making sure the simmering water doesn't touch the bottom of the top pan holding the eggs. Gently whisk until the eggs have become slightly thicker than unwhipped 35% cream. Don't overcook or the eggs will curdle.

Remove the pan holding the eggs from the heat and slowly whisk in the melted butter until the mixture thickens.

Add the remaining 1 tsp. (5 mL) lemon juice, salt, pepper, and mint. If the hollandaise is too thick, stir in a little bit of warm water. Keep warm in a thermos bottle for up to 20 minutes. If the hollandaise has started to separate, whisk it together before serving.

The nymph Mentha, a symbol of hospitality in Greek mythology, angered Pluto's wife, Persephone, who turned her into the fragrant herb, mint. Although mint is cultivated in North America, Europe, and Asia, it grows wild throughout the world.

Gardiane de Boeuf

SERVES 6 TO 8

I first tasted a version of this simple stew near Marseilles. It was July and the cook served it lukewarm with a room temperature vegetable tian (baked vegetables). It's equally good served piping hot in the fall and winter. Like most stews, it's better if it's made the day before serving. Your biggest job will be slicing the onions. If you use a food processor, you'll be able to assemble this dish in 15 minutes flat—not much kitchen time for a rustic stew that never fails to elicit oohs and aahs. I would start the dinner with Bagna Cauda (see page 63). Serve the stew with either Polenta Fries (see page 157) or Smashed Potatoes (see page 159) and finish with Antiguan Caramelized Bananas over Vanilla Ice Cream (see page 175).

4 lbs. (1.8 kg) point of the rump, cut in
¼-inch (6-mm) slices (see Cook's Tip)
4 lbs. (1.8 kg) yellow cooking onions, peeled
and thinly sliced
4 large minced garlic cloves

1 generous Tbsp. (15 mL) herbes de Provence
kosher salt and freshly ground black pepper
1½ cups (360 mL) dry red wine
⅓ generous cup (80 mL) Dijon mustard
⅓ cup (80 mL) olive oil

Preheat the oven to 350°F (175°C).

Arrange one slightly overlapping layer of meat slices in the bottom of a 14-cup (3.5-L) casserole dish that has a lid.

Sprinkle the meat with a heaping ½ tsp. (2.5 mL) herbes de Provence and with generous amounts of salt and pepper. Cover the meat completely with onions. Continue layering in this sequence to within ¾ inch (1.9 cm) of the top of the casserole, making sure to finish with a layer of onions.

Pour the wine over the layers, cover, and bake for 3 hours. The stew will have reduced in height by 3 or more inches (7.5 cm).

In a small bowl, mix the mustard and oil. After 3 hours of baking, remove casserole dish from oven and smooth the mustard mixture over the top of the stew. Cover and bake for another hour.

Serve directly from the casserole dish into individual bowls with Polenta Fries (see page 157) or Smashed Potatoes (see page 159), and buttered green beans with plenty of baguette to soak up the juices.

COOK'S TIP

William DeGroot, a third generation butcher at Olliffe Meats in Toronto, gave me the following instructions for you to pass on to your butcher: Order the point of the rump, also called the bottom round or silverback. Have your butcher remove all the outside connective tissue, but leave all the inside bits of fat for flavour. Then ask your butcher to cut ¼-inch (6-mm) slices with the grain. You will end up with slices 2½ to 3 inches (6.2 to 7.5 cm) wide and 5 to 6 inches (12.5 to 15 cm) long.

Polenta Fries p. 157

Broccoli Purée with Lemon-Garlic
Breadcrumbs p. 168

Stuffed Pork Chops with Pomegranate-Maple Glaze

SERVES 6

Homey pork chops become sophisticated with the addition of dried porcini mushrooms and the combination of maple syrup and pomegranate molasses. Your butcher can cut the pockets in the meat that will be stuffed with the mushroom mixture. Make sure he starts from the bone and cuts outward from there. I have put instructions in the method section of the recipe, if you wish to do it yourself. If you want to be fancy, ask your butcher to leave a longer bone on each chop and French it.

6 rib loin pork chops, 1½-inch (3.8-cm) thick
5 Tbsp. (75 mL) maple syrup
3 Tbsp. (45 mL) pomegranate molasses
1 oz. (28 g) dried porcini mushrooms soaked in hot water for a half hour
1½ Tbsp. (22.5 mL) canola oil, and extra for sautéing the chops
3 Tbsp. (45 mL) minced shallots

1 Tbsp. (15 mL) minced fresh sage
¾ Tbsp. (11.25 mL) minced fresh thyme
¾ cup (180 mL) fresh fine breadcrumbs (see Cook's Tip, page 168)
¼ tsp. (1.2 mL) kosher salt
large pinch freshly ground black pepper
kosher salt and fresh ground black pepper, to taste, for the chops

Preheat the oven to 375°F (190°C).

Cut a large horizontal pocket into each chop, running a very sharp knife along the top of the bone and as far as possible into and across the flesh of the chop. Don't cut all the way through the meat.

Mix the maple syrup and the pomegranate molasses in a small saucepan. Bring to a boil over high. Reduce heat to low and simmer for 3 minutes. Remove from heat.

Drain the mushrooms, pat dry, and mince. Pour the oil into a nonstick frying pan. Add the shallots, and sauté on medium heat for about 3 to 5 minutes or until the shallots are soft but not coloured.

Add the mushrooms to the onions and continue sautéing for another 2 to 3 minutes. Add the sage, thyme, breadcrumbs, salt, and pepper to taste. Cook for one minute and let cool.

Spoon the stuffing into the pockets of the 6 room-temperature chops.

Generously salt and pepper both sides of the chops and sauté in a little canola oil over medium-high for about 2 minutes per side or until golden brown.

Brush both sides of each chop with the glaze. Transfer to a baking dish and place in the oven for 18 to 20 minutes, brushing every 5 minutes with the glaze. Boil down any remaining glaze until it is reduced to 1 to 2 Tbsp. (15 to 30 mL). Remove the chops from the oven, and give them a final brush with the thickened glaze. Let the chops sit for 10 minutes to finish the cooking cycle. Drizzle with a little of the hot pan juices before serving.

COOK'S TIP

Pomegranate molasses is available in gourmet and Middle Eastern grocery stores and in some large grocery chains. Undiluted pomegranate juice concentrate can be substituted for the molasses. Pomegranate juice is not concentrated enough to produce the intense flavour this dish needs.

Roasted Chicken on a Bed of Potatoes, Mushrooms and Shallots

One-dish meals are great for family dinners and casual weekend entertaining. They can be served right from the roasting pan or, if you're feeling a little more ambitious, spoon the vegetables onto a favourite serving dish, arrange the chicken on top, and decorate with sprigs of rosemary.

three ¼-inch-thick (6-mm) slices smoked
    bacon, cut in ¼-inch (6-mm) cubes
9 to 10 large garlic cloves, peeled
2 Tbsp. (30 mL) freshly squeezed lemon juice
3 to 4 Tbsp. (45 to 60 mL) olive oil
1 Tbsp. (15 mL) fresh minced rosemary
1½ tsp. (7.5 mL) kosher salt
⅛ tsp. (0.5 mL) freshly ground black pepper
12 shallots, peeled
2 large or 4 medium Portobello mushrooms

20 to 25 mini potatoes, 1½ to 2 inches (3.8
    to 5 cm) in length
3 sprigs fresh rosemary + more for garnishing
    the finished dish
3 chicken legs
3 chicken half breasts with bone in
12 to 16 cherry tomatoes (optional)
coarsely ground sea salt and black pepper to
    taste

Sauté the bacon over medium heat until it has rendered its fat and all the cubes are cooked through. Drain and reserve.

Finely grate 3 to 4 garlic cloves in a small bowl and mix with the lemon juice, 1 Tbsp. (15 mL) olive oil, minced rosemary, ½ tsp. (2.5 mL) salt, and pepper.

Thoroughly rub the mixture into the chicken and let marinate at room temperature while preparing the vegetables, or in the refrigerator for 1½ to 2 hours.

Preheat the oven to 450°F (230°C).

Bring the chicken to room temperature if it has been in the refrigerator.

Scrape the black gills from the insides of the mushroom caps using a teaspoon, and cut the mushrooms into 1- to 1½-inch (2.5- to 3.9-cm) pieces. Cut the potatoes into halves or quarters, depending on size. Mince 6 garlic cloves.

Toss together the shallots, mushrooms, potatoes, 3 small sprigs rosemary, 2 to 3 Tbsp. (30 to 45 mL) olive oil, and the minced garlic cloves. Spoon into a shallow baking dish large enough to hold all the chicken in one layer.

Place the chicken legs on the vegetables and roast for 10 minutes. Add the chicken breasts and roast for 25 to 30 minutes, depending on the size of the chicken pieces. The chicken is cooked when the juices run clear, not pink.

Transfer the chicken to a dish and loosely tent with tin foil to keep warm.

Put the vegetables back in the oven until the potatoes are cooked through, another 10 to 15 minutes. This will also allow the chicken to rest. Add the cherry tomatoes, if using, in the last 5 to 7 minutes of cooking time.

Discard the cooked rosemary sprigs and serve the chicken directly from the baking dish or spoon the vegetables onto a serving dish with a small lip. Put the chicken on top of the vegetables and top with the bacon, some fresh rosemary sprigs, and a sprinkle of coarsely ground sea salt and black pepper.

COOK'S TIP

If you decide to roast just chicken breasts, remember to add the "leg time" of 10 minutes to the roasting of the vegetables.

"There's rosemary, that's for remembrance! Pray love, remember."

—William Shakespeare

Bangers and Potato-Apple Mash with Onion Red Wine Gravy

SERVES 4

One of our kids' favourite comfort dinners, this can be made ahead of time. Roast the sausages, make the mash, and cook the onion gravy to the point at which you add the sausages. A half hour before dinner, add the sausages to the onions and heat up the potatoes over a bain marie (see page 42). I'd be tempted to start with the Arugula, Fig and Chèvre Salad (see page 104). You may want to finish with citrus sorbet and Ginger Biscotti (see page 181)..

8 large pork sausages
1 to 2 tsp. (5 to 10 mL) vegetable oil
¼ cup (60 mL) chicken stock

POTATOES
3 large baking potatoes
1 to 2 tsp. (5 to 10 mL) vegetable oil
2 Granny Smith apples, peeled, cored, and cut
   into ½-inch (1.2-cm) cubes
2 tsp. (10 mL) finely minced fresh rosemary
1 cup (240 mL) homogenized milk
3 to 4 Tbsp. (45 to 60 mL) softened unsalted
   butter
1 tsp. (5 mL) kosher salt

ONION SAUCE
2 Tbsp. (30 mL) vegetable oil
4 large yellow cooking onions, peeled and
   thinly sliced
1 large garlic clove, minced
2 sprigs fresh rosemary, 4 inches (10 cm) long
1 cup (240 mL) chicken stock
¾ cup (180 mL) red wine
1 Tbsp. (15 mL) unsalted butter

Preheat the oven to 400°F (200°C). Rub the sausages with 1 to 2 tsp. (5 to 10 mL) vegetable oil and place on a small baking sheet with a lip. Roast for approximately 30 minutes, turning frequently, until golden brown on all sides. Remove the sausages from the baking sheet and drain off most of the fat. Deglaze the pan with ¼ cup (60 mL) of chicken stock. Set aside.

FOR THE POTATOES

Peel, cube, and boil the potatoes until tender. Drain the potatoes and place them on a separate baking sheet in the oven with the sausages for 5 to 7 minutes; this will steam off the excess moisture. Remove from oven and force the potatoes through a ricer; set aside. (If you don't have a ricer, return the potatoes to the pot you boiled them in and mash until just smooth.)

In a nonstick frying pan, heat 1 to 2 tsp. (5 to 10 mL) of vegetable oil. Add the apple and minced rosemary and sauté, stirring often, until the apples are light golden but still retain their shape.

Just before serving, warm the milk. Over medium heat, gently mix the butter, salt, and milk into the potatoes. Add more butter and milk as needed. Fold in the apples.

Pour the vegetable oil into a frying pan and immediately add the onions. Turn the heat to medium-low and sauté for 20 to 25 minutes, stirring occasionally, until the onions range from light to dark golden in colour. Add the garlic and continue sautéing for another 2 minutes. Toss in the rosemary sprigs, 1 cup (240 mL) chicken stock, and the wine. Simmer gently for 15 to 20 minutes or until the liquid is reduced by half. Remove the rosemary sprigs, add the sausages and deglazed pan juices, and cook for another 10 minutes. Stir in 1 Tbsp. (15 mL) butter just before serving.

Mound the potatoes on a serving dish. Top with sausages and pour the caramelized onion sauce over top.

COOK'S TIP

Pork sausages taste great with the Potato-Apple Mash but if you're feeling adventurous, try venison, or Toulouse or spicy sausages.

Rosemary oil, said to aid poor circulation, is often used in bath products, while a tissane made of rosemary leaves steeped in boiling water for about 5 minutes, will help with digestive problems.

Foolproof New York Strip Steaks with Two Accompaniments

SERVES 4 TO 6

It's easy to cook a rare steak without burning the outside but it becomes a little more of a challenge if you like your meat medium-rare or medium. That's why I like to finish my steaks in a hot oven. It's imperative that your meat be at room temperature before you start cooking and that you give the meat time to rest after it's done, otherwise the timing I suggest will be off.

    four 10 to 11 oz. (285 to 310 g) New York
        strip steaks, about 1¼-inch (3-cm) thick
    olive oil
    2 to 4 tsp. (10 to 20 mL) kosher salt
    coarsely ground black pepper

Preheat the oven to 450°F (230°C).

Brush the steaks with olive oil and sprinkle both sides of each steak with kosher salt and a grinding of fresh black pepper.

Heat a grill pan or cast iron pan on high until very hot. For rare steaks, sear each side for 2 minutes. (If you are using a grill pan, rotate 90° halfway through searing time on each side to create cross-hatching.) For medium-rare steaks, transfer to the oven-proof pan and roast in the oven for 5 to 6 minutes. Add 1½ more minutes for medium.

In either case, transfer the steaks to a cutting board when finished cooking and let rest for 10 minutes.

Serve as one large steak per person or cut into ¼- to ½-inch (6-mm to 1.2-cm) slices and fan on a serving dish.

Stilton Cream Sauce

MAKES ¾ CUP (180 mL)

A little goes a long way with this rich and creamy sauce, a favourite with the men in the family. It's also delicious poured over cooked cauliflower, broccoli, or potatoes.

1 Tbsp. (15 mL) minced shallots
½ cup (120 mL) 10% cream
1½ oz. (42 g) crumbled Stilton cheese
⅛ tsp. (0.5 mL) freshly ground white pepper
1 Tbsp. (15 mL) dry white wine

Put the shallots and cream into a small saucepan and bring to a simmer over medium-low heat until the shallots are soft and the cream has thickened slightly, about 5 minutes. Lower the heat, add the cheese, and stir until the cheese has melted and the sauce coats a spoon. Season with white pepper and stir in the wine. Heat for 30 seconds. Serve warm.

Cognac Butter

MAKES 12 PIECES

A pat of this compound butter over a grilled steak is a beautiful thing. It will keep in the freezer for two months.

½ cup (120 mL) softened unsalted butter
½ heaping tsp. (2.5 mL) grated garlic
1 tsp. (5 mL) minced fresh tarragon
1½ tsp. (7.5 mL) minced fresh Italian parsley
1 Tbsp. + 1 tsp. (20 mL) cognac

In a small bowl and using a fork, mash together the butter, garlic, tarragon, and parsley. Slowly dribble in the cognac and continue to mash and mix the ingredients until well blended. The cognac will initially bead on the butter mixture. Persevere and it will slowly blend into a solid mass.

Spoon the butter in a line onto a piece of tin foil. Use the foil to roll the butter into a 1½- × 5-inch (3.7- × 12.5-cm) long log. Refrigerate until hard before cutting into ⅜-inch (9.5-mm) slices. Serve disks of butter on the warm steaks.

Peixe Assado No Forno

SERVES 4

Isabel De Sousa makes this typical Portuguese recipe with salt cod (see Cook's Tip). But if she's in a hurry, she will substitute fresh fish. I've given you the choice of using fresh or canned tomatoes, depending on the season. If you don't want to be in the kitchen at the last moment, boil the potatoes, sear the fish, and make the sauce ahead of time. Refrigerate separately, but bring to room temperature before you put the various parts together. Heat up the sauce, ladle it over the potatoes and fish, and place the dish in the oven.

3 large Yukon Gold or white potatoes
3 lbs. (1.35 kg) tomatoes, cored and sliced ¼-inch (6-mm) thick or two 28-oz. (796-mL) cans whole peeled tomatoes in juice
3 Tbsp. (45 mL) olive oil
1 large yellow cooking onion, peeled and thinly sliced, about 1 cup (240 mL)
2 garlic cloves peeled and grated
3 bay leaves
10 basil leaves (6 whole, 4 julienned)

½ cup (120 mL) dry white wine
½ tsp. (2.5 mL) salt
⅛ tsp. (0.5 mL) freshly ground pepper
four 7- to 8-oz. (200- to 225-g) pieces skinless Atlantic cod, Alaskan black cod, or any other thick, flaky white fish
¼ cup (60 mL) finely chopped fresh Italian parsley
1 to 2 tsp. (5 to10 mL) finely grated lemon zest

Preheat the oven to 375°F (190°C).

Peel the potatoes and cut into slices ⅛-inch (3-mm) thick. Boil in salted water until just barely cooked, about 5 to 6 minutes. Drain and reserve. If using canned tomatoes, drain and reserve the juice from the cans for another use. Slice the tomatoes, fresh or tinned, reserving the juice and pulp that comes out of them.

Heat 2 Tbsp. (30 mL) olive oil over medium heat in a deep frying pan, large enough to hold the onions and tomatoes. Sauté the onions for 4 to 5 minutes until softened but not coloured. Stir in the garlic and continue cooking for another 30 seconds. Add the tomatoes, reserved juice and pulp, bay leaves, 6 whole basil leaves, wine, salt, and pepper to the frying pan and simmer for 20 minutes.

Season the fish with salt and pepper and quickly sear both sides in 1 Tbsp. (15 mL) olive oil over high heat (about 1 to 1½ minutes each side).

Arrange an overlapping layer of potato slices in a 10 ½- × 6 ½-inch (26.5- × 16.5-cm) casserole dish 2 to 3 inches (5 to 7.5 cm) deep that is more than large enough to hold the fish in one layer.

Place the seared fish over the potatoes, discard the bay leaves from the tomato sauce, and spoon the sauce over fish and potatoes.

Bake, uncovered, for about 15 to 20 minutes, making sure not to overcook the fish. A good guide for baking or roasting fish is to allow 10 minutes in the oven for each 1 inch (2.5 cm) of thickness, cooking at 350° to 375°F (175° to 190°C). Allow a little bit more time if all the components are at room temperature.

Remove from the oven, sprinkle with parsley, julienned basil, and lemon zest. Serve with thick slices of baguette to soak up the sauce.

COOK'S TIP

If you want to make this in the traditional manner, you'll need to soak the salt cod in cold water for 24 to 36 hours, changing the water periodically. Then carefully poach it over medium heat for 15 to 20 minutes, making sure the water doesn't come to a boil. Layer the potatoes, fish, and tomatoes. Bake until heated through.

Salt cod can be bought in Portuguese and Spanish fish and grocery stores. It can also occasionally be found in gourmet markets or in maritime specialty food stores.

Orange Steamed Mussels with Tomatoes and Breadcrumbs

SERVES 8 AS AN APPETIZER OR 4 AS A MAIN

Atlantic mussels are at their best in the spring; Pacific mussels are best from November to April; and Mediterranean mussels are best in the summer. This means you can get delicious mussels year-round. Use a regular orange if blood oranges aren't in season, but you will miss having a beautiful, rosy-coloured broth. If you are having the mussels as a main course, consider doing what the Belgians do and have some French fries on the side. With or without the fries, you will still need a baguette to sop up the broth.

1 Tbsp. (15 mL) unsalted butter
1 cup (240 mL) coarse fresh breadcrumbs
2 to 3 Tbsp. (30 to 45 mL) coarsely chopped Italian parsley + 2 large stalks with leaves
2 Tbsp. (30 mL) vegetable oil
⅓ cup (80 mL) minced cooking onion, about 1 small onion
1 large stalk celery, sliced ¼-inch (6-mm) thick

2 cloves garlic, minced
1 cup (240 mL) Sauvignon Blanc wine
four ¼-inch (6-mm) slices blood orange, peeled if not organic
4 lbs. (1.8 kg) mussels, cleaned and debearded
20 cherry tomatoes, cut in half
1 baguette

Melt the butter in a small sauté pan over medium heat. Add the breadcrumbs and sauté for approximately 5 minutes or until dark golden. Remove from the heat, toss in the chopped parsley, and reserve.

Heat the vegetable oil in a pot large enough to hold the mussels. Sauté the onion over medium-low heat for about 2 minutes. Add the celery and continue cooking for another 3 or 4 minutes or until it has just begun to soften but not brown. Throw in the garlic and sauté 1 minute more. Pour in the wine and add the orange slices and parsley stalks.

Add the mussels and tomatoes to the pot. Cover and cook over high heat for about 5 minutes or until the mussel shells have opened. Discard any that remain closed.

Ladle the mussels, celery, onion, tomatoes, oranges, and broth into 4 bowls (or 8 if serving as an appetizer). Sprinkle liberally with breadcrumbs and serve with slices of baguette.

COOK'S TIP

To keep mussels fresh, wrap them in damp paper towel or newspaper, then in a plastic bag before refrigerating them. Rinse them in cool water before cooking and discard any that remain open.

Rosemary Skewered Grilled Shrimp on Summer Vegetables

SERVES 4 AS AN APPETIZER OR 2 AS A LIGHT MAIN

Low in calories, but bursting with taste, you'll find yourself making this all summer long. The beans can be boiled and shocked in cold water a few hours before you plan to sit down. The rest of this light and healthy dish can be prepared in 25 minutes, including the marinating of the shrimp. For a late summer weekend lunch or casual dinner, start with the Red Pepper and Corn Soup (see page 84). Serve the soup and shrimps with Rosemary Olive Oil Grissini (see page 26) or Cheddar Roll Cluster (see page 21). The Plum, Cardamom and Hazelnut Crisp (see page 191) would be an excellent finish.

2 Tbsp. (30 mL) olive oil
1 large clove of garlic, finely minced
kosher salt and freshly ground black pepper
12 raw jumbo shrimp, peeled
4 sturdy rosemary branches, approximately
   6- to 7-inches (15- to 18-cm) long
2 large handfuls of green beans, preferably
   haricots vert
3 large handfuls of baby arugula

½ English cucumber, sliced ⅛-inch
   (3-mm) thick
2-4 large tomatoes, different colours if
   possible, sliced ¼-inch (6-mm) thick
1 avocado, cut in half
½ lemon
balsamic vinegar
robust extra-virgin olive oil

Mix 2 Tbsp. (30 mL) olive oil, garlic, salt, and pepper in a low-rimmed dish. Toss in the shrimp to marinate while preparing the vegetables.

Pull the leaves off the bottom three-quarters of the rosemary branches and soak them in cool water for 10 minutes. Pat dry. Boil beans in slightly salted water until just cooked, about 7 to 10 minutes. Plunge into cold water to stop cooking and retain colour; drain. On a flat serving dish or on individual plates, layer with arugula and beans, followed by cucumber and tomatoes.

Thread three shrimp on each rosemary branch. Grill on a barbecue or in a grill pan for about 2½ minutes per side. Squeeze with lemon juice after turning.

While the shrimp are cooking, use a teaspoon to scoop out pieces of avocado and place on top of the tomatoes.

Drizzle the vegetables with balsamic vinegar and a robust olive oil. Sprinkle with salt and pepper, top with the shrimp, and serve immediately.

COOK'S TIP

Come colder weather, drain and rinse a can or two of cannellini beans, warm them up in a saucepan, and toss with some minced red onion, red pepper, pitted black olives, and a few leaves of basil or arugula. Pour a few spoonfuls of olive oil over the mixture and squeeze lemon juice over top. Season with salt and pepper, toss, and use as a bed for the shrimp.

Pasta al Pesto

SERVES 6 TO 8 AS AN APPETIZER OR 4 AS A MAIN

I had pasta very much like this at my friend Susan Doull's house in the hill town of Sermonetta, just south of Rome. An antipasto of some good proscuitto with figs or peaches and buffalo mozzarella, followed by the pasta, makes a wonderful weekend lunch. A green salad, then a bowl of fresh fruit and Ginger Biscotti (see page 181) will keep you at the table until evening. When I serve Pasta al Pesto as a first course, I often follow with the Foolproof New York Strip Steak (see page 148) and the Roasted Leeks, Peppers and Tomatoes (see page 165). Bear in mind that different shapes of pasta will need more or less of the sauce.

2 large handfuls green beans
1 lb 2 oz. (500 g) Troffie pasta or other 3- to 4-inch (7.5- to 10-cm) long and slightly twisted pasta
1 cup (240 mL) Tuscan Pesto (see page 75) or good quality store-bought pesto
1 Tbsp. + 1 tsp. (20 mL) extra-virgin olive oil, if using Tuscan Pesto, or more if needed (see Cook's Tips)

1 Tbsp. (15 mL) freshly squeezed lemon juice, or more
kosher salt
½ cup (120 mL) freshly grated Parmigiano Reggiano

Boil the beans for about 7 to 10 minutes or until cooked but still crisp. Refresh under cold water to preserve the colour, drain, and cut into thirds.

Cook the pasta in salted water until al dente. Meanwhile, in a warm serving bowl, mix the pesto with the olive oil and lemon juice (see Cook's Tips for consistency of sauce).

Toss in the drained pasta and green beans. Season with salt to taste.

Serve in warmed bowls with a sprinkling of Parmigiano Reggiano.

COOK'S TIPS

1. Homemade pesto is usually thicker than its store-bought equivalent. Even commercial pesto will differ from maker to maker. For this recipe, the pesto should have the consistency of a puréed tomato sauce.

2. In Italy, troffie, curled pasta about two inches (5 cm) long, is the proper shape to be tossed with pesto. You should be able to find it in specialty stores but if you can't, substitute any short, curled pasta.

Polenta Fries

SERVES 6 TO 8

These fries are a little fiddly to make, but well worth the effort. If you are making polenta for another dish, consider doubling the recipe so you can have the fries later in the week. It's important to add the polenta quickly to the water or stock. If you do a slow pour, you will end up with lumps throughout the cornmeal. A nonstick frying pan will give you pale golden fries while a stainless steel or cast iron pan will produce darker ones. I love these fries with the Stuffed Pork Chops with Pomegranate-Maple Glaze (see page 143) or the Gardiane de Boeuf (see page 141).

4 cups (1 L) water or chicken stock
½ tsp. (2.5 mL) kosher salt
1¼ cups (250 g) fine cornmeal or polenta
1 cup (240 mL) freshly grated Parmigiano Reggiano

¾ to 1 tsp. (3.75 to 5 mL) fresh minced rosemary
olive oil for greasing pan and frying
sea salt to sprinkle on fries

Bring the water or chicken stock to a simmer in a large pot over high heat. Add the salt. Remove from the heat and quickly pour in the cornmeal, stirring constantly with a wooden spoon.

Return the pot to medium-low heat and cook, stirring frequently, for about 30 to 40 minutes or until the polenta pulls away from the sides of the pot.

Stir in the cheese and rosemary and spoon the polenta into a lightly greased medium-sized baking dish. Smooth the top with a spatula. The polenta should be ½-inch (1.2-cm) thick.

When the polenta is cool, cover with plastic wrap and refrigerate, if you are not going to prepare the fries immediately.

Return the polenta to room temperature an hour before proceeding with the recipe. Flip the polenta out of the dish and onto a cutting board and cut into batons approximately ½ inch × 2½ inches (1.2 cm × 6.25 cm).

Heat a film of olive oil over medium heat if you are using a nonstick frying pan, otherwise add about ⅛ inch (3 mm) of oil. Fry the polenta batons on all four sides until golden brown. Drain on paper towels and arrange on a serving dish. Sprinkle with sea salt before serving.

Smashed Potatoes

Potato Fennel Rosti p. 161

Dilled Potatoes p. 160

Smashed Potatoes

SERVES 4

It's impossible to write an exact recipe for smashed potatoes: you will find the combination you like and it will be yours! The original recipe doesn't call for lemon juice or chives—both additions are our daughter Devin's suggestions. Good ones, I think.

twelve 3-inch (7.5-cm) diameter boiling
   potatoes
½ tsp. (2.5 mL) kosher salt
extra-virgin olive oil
coarse sea salt
freshly squeezed lemon juice
minced fresh chives

Boil the potatoes in a pot of salted water until cooked through, about 20 to 25 minutes. Drain and wrap in a kitchen towel. Using the heel of your hand, press gently on the potatoes until the skin breaks and they are lightly squashed.

Transfer the potatoes to a serving platter. Drizzle very generously with olive oil and sprinkle with coarse sea salt. Squeeze a touch of lemon juice over the potatoes and sprinkle with chives before serving.

Dilled Potatoes

SERVES 4

During my childhood, when my Dad was the military attaché at the Canadian Embassy in Stockholm, my mother learned to cook quite a few Swedish dishes. Dilled potatoes (photo page 158) were one of our favourites. In Sweden, these are served with gravlax (marinated raw salmon). But dilled potatoes are also delicious with grilled wild salmon, Foolproof New York Strip Steaks with Stilton Sauce (see page 148), or on their own, generously sprinkled with crumbled crispy bacon accompanied by a wedge of St. Andre cheese.

20 baby new potatoes
¼ cup (60 mL) unsalted butter
up to ¾ cup (180 mL) water
¼ tsp. (1.2 mL) kosher salt
3 to 4 Tbsp. (45 to 60 mL) finely chopped
   fresh dill
coarse sea salt

Put the potatoes, butter, half the water, and kosher salt in a large saucepan with a tight fitting lid. Cover and steam over medium-low heat, shaking occasionally. Check periodically to see if more water is needed.

There should be a thin film of butter over the potatoes by the time they are cooked through, roughly 20 minutes.

Add dill and thoroughly toss with the potatoes before turning into a serving bowl. Sprinkle with sea salt and serve immediately.

COOK'S TIP

When buying fresh dill, look for soft green, perky fronds. Beware of wilted, yellowish coloured dill. Dried dill has very little flavour.

Potato Fennel Rosti

These rosti (photo page 158) seem to go with just about any meat or fish. The fennel lightens up the mixture and provides a clean, fresh taste that is a little out of the ordinary. If you mix vegetable oil and butter when sautéing, the rosti will have a richer taste and darker golden exterior.

½ to ⅔ large fennel bulb
1 small cooking onion
3 to 4 large new potatoes
1 large egg
2 Tbsp. (30 mL) all-purpose flour
¾ tsp. (4 mL) kosher salt

⅛ heaping tsp. (0.5 mL) freshly ground black pepper
vegetable oil for frying
½ cup (120 mL) crème fraîche
1 Tbsp. (15 mL) minced fresh chives

Coarsely grate the fennel, onion, and potatoes by hand or in a food processor. Drain in a colander, pressing down on the mixture with a large flat spoon. Spoon into a bowl and pat dry with paper towels. Mix in the egg, flour, salt, and pepper.

Heat a thin layer of oil in a nonstick frying pan over medium-high heat and scoop ¼-cup (60-mL) amounts of the rosti mixture into the pan. Flatten with the bottom of a measuring cup until the rosti are about 4 inches (10 cm) in diameter. Add as many rosti as can be comfortably contained in the pan without touching.

Cook until golden, about 3 to 4 minutes, flip, and repeat on the other side. The rosti should be crisp and golden on the outside and soft inside. If they are getting too dark, complete the cooking in the oven at 350°F (175°C) for 5 to 10 minutes.

Keep the finished cakes warm in the oven. They will not overcook. Mix the crème fraîche and the chives together and serve in a bowl with the warm rosti.

Crispy Carrot Parsnip Cakes with Spinach-Yogurt Sauce

MAKES 6 TO 8 CAKES

The warm exterior crunchiness of the carrot parsnip cakes pairs well with the cool bright flavour of the Spinach-Yogurt Sauce. They make a light vegetarian supper but can also be served with the Foolproof New York Strip Steaks (see page 148), The Stuffed Pork Chops with Pomegranate-Maple Glaze (see page 143), or with any grilled fish. If you don't have time to drain the yogurt, assemble the sauce at the last moment.

SPINACH-YOGURT SAUCE

3 cups (720 mL) loosely packed baby spinach
⅛ tsp. (1.5 mL) kosher salt
¼ tsp. (1.2 mL) hot paprika
1 garlic clove, finely minced, about ⅛ tsp. (0.5 mL)
1 cup (240 mL) plain yogurt, drained in a sieve for at least 1 hour to yield ⅔ cups (160 mL)

CARROT PARSNIP CAKES

4 cups (950 mL) peeled and coarsely grated carrot (about 18 bunch carrots)
2 cups (475 mL) peeled, cored, and coarsely grated parsnips (about 3 to 4 large parsnips)
1 tsp. (5 mL) garam masala
¼ tsp. (1.2 mL) ground cinnamon
½ tsp. (2.5 mL) ground coriander
½ tsp. (2.5 mL) kosher salt
⅛ tsp. (0.5 mL) freshly ground black pepper
4 large eggs
up to 1 Tbsp. (15 mL) all-purpose flour
¼ to ½ cup (60 to 120 mL) fresh breadcrumbs (see Cook's Tip, page 168)
2 tsp. (10 mL) unsalted butter + 1 Tbsp. (15 mL) canola oil for searing cakes

Preheat the oven to 400°F (200°C).

FOR SPINACH-YOGURT SAUCE

Blanch the spinach and salt in a pot of boiling water for 1 minute. Drain and cool. Press as much water out as possible and mince with a sharp knife.

In a medium bowl, stir the spinach, hot paprika, and garlic into the drained yogurt. Taste and add more paprika or garlic, if you wish. Transfer to a serving bowl and refrigerate until serving.

FOR CARROT PARSNIP CAKES

Put the grated carrots and parsnips into a bowl large enough to hold all the ingredients. Whisk the garam masala, cinnamon, coriander, and salt and pepper into the eggs; pour egg mixture over the carrots and parsnips. Toss well before sprinkling with enough breadcrumbs and flour to bind. Mix with your hands, form into 8 patties and press lightly to extract some of the liquid. They will be quite fragile. Make sure each patty is an equal height throughout. Reserve on a plate until ready to cook.

Melt 2 tsp. (10 mL) butter and 1 Tbsp. (15 mL) canola oil in a frying pan on medium heat until it has stopped bubbling. Quickly add as many cakes as can be comfortably contained in the pan without touching. Fry both sides of the cakes for about 3 minutes per side or until golden brown. Add more butter and lower the heat if needed.

Place the seared cakes on a baking sheet and bake in the oven for about 15 minutes. Pierce with a knife to make sure the vegetables are soft. Place on a serving dish and serve with a bowl of Spinach-Yogurt Sauce on the side.

COOK'S TIP

Garam Masala is a blend of dry-roasted ground spices that add a warm note to any dish. The name literally means "hot or warm spice," and although there are many variations, the traditional mix uses cinnamon, cloves, nutmeg, mace, black pepper, and cardamom. Originally from northern India, it can be found in the spice section of most grocery stores.

It wasn't until the sixteenth-century that the English language differentiated between carrots and parsnips. Parsnips, which have a pleasantly sweet flavour, are at their best in the fall and winter seasons. Look for hard, smooth roots that aren't shriveled or spotted with bruises.

Carrots and Cipollini Onions en Papillote

SERVES 4

Don't use the so-called baby carrots found pre-packaged in grocery stores. Instead buy the first carrots of the season, or buy bunch carrots that can be halved horizontally. You can put the vegetables in one large package, or make individual ones for your guests—that way they will each smell the beautiful aroma of the honey-roasted carrots and onions.

20 small young carrots or 12 bunch carrots	two 3- to 4-inch (7.5 to 10 cm) sprigs fresh
16 to 20 cipollini onions	thyme, leaves removed
¼ cup (60 mL) dry white wine	kosher salt and freshly ground white pepper
1½ tsp (7.5 mL) wildflower honey	1 to 2 tsp. (5 to 10 mL) unsalted butter

Preheat the oven to 375°F (190°C).

Wash but don't peel the small young carrots, leaving on ½ inch (1.2 cm) of greenery. If you are using bunch carrots, peel and cut them in half lengthwise.

Drop the onions in boiling water and cook for 3 minutes. Drain and plunge into cold water to cool. Peel the skins off and reserve.

Mix the wine and honey in a saucepan over medium meat until the honey melts; set aside.

Create 4 pouches with pieces of tin foil or parchment paper.

Divide the carrots and onions evenly onto the 4 pieces of foil, sprinkle with thyme, and drizzle with the wine-and-honey mixture. Sprinkle with salt and pepper and dot with butter.

Tightly seal the pouches and bake for 20 to 25 minutes. A large single pouch may need 5 more minutes. When done, remove from oven and serve in the pouch, or in bowls or on a platter.

COOK'S TIP

Cipollini onions are small, flat-topped onions used in Italian cooking. If you can't find any, substitute pearl onions, which should be boiled for just 2 minutes.

Thyme, a member of the mint family is indigenous to the Mediterranean but is used in cooking worldwide. Unlike most herbs, it can withstand a long cooking period and is therefore an indispensable herb for stews.

Roasted Leeks, Peppers and Tomatoes

SERVES 4

I make this when I've had a long day and I'm looking for a quick vegetable dish to serve with meat, poultry, or fish. You can add quartered new baby potatoes to the leeks and peppers. If you're looking for a vegetarian one-dish dinner, toss ¼-inch (6-mm) slices of Tallegio, a soft Italian cheese, or chunks of chèvre over the top of the vegetables during the last few minutes of cooking.

4 large leeks (white and pale green part)	kosher salt
1 medium to large yellow bell pepper	16 to 20 cherry tomatoes
1 medium to large red bell pepper	1 to 2 tsp. (5 to 10 mL) chopped fresh thyme
olive oil	freshly ground black pepper

Preheat the oven to 425°F (220°C).

Cut the leeks in half lengthwise and soak in cold water for 10 minutes to remove sand. Remove from water and pat dry.

Wash the peppers and cut into 8 pieces each, making sure to remove all the seeds.

Rub the leeks and the peppers with oil. Sprinkle with salt, and roast for 18 to 20 minutes.

Rub the tomatoes with oil and add to the peppers and leeks. Sprinkle with the thyme and pepper, and roast for another 7 minutes.

Transfer to a platter and serve immediately.

Wild Mushroom and Ricotta Strata

SERVES 8 TO 12

A whole grilled snapper or sea bream, or a garlic and orange-infused pork roast would be all you'd need to serve with this strata. It can be put together the evening before and baked the evening of. If you use brie instead of ricotta, you can dispense with the fish or meat and serve it with a green salad, a baguette, and a good bottle of red wine.

1 large Portobello mushroom, 4 to 5 oz. (113 to 140 g) (see Cook's Tips)

7 oz. (200 g) brown button mushrooms

4 oz. (113 g) chanterelle mushrooms

9 oz. (255 g) shiitake mushrooms

½ oz. (14 g) dried porcini mushrooms, soaked in hot water for 20 minutes (see Cook's Tips, page 167)

4 medium to large leeks, white and pale green part, sliced ¼-inch (6-mm) thick

1 Tbsp. (15 mL) olive oil for the mushrooms + 1½ Tbsp. (22.5 mL) olive oil for the leeks

1 Tbsp. (15 mL) unsalted butter

1½ tsp. (7.5 mL) minced garlic

¼ tsp. (1.2 mL) minced fresh thyme

½ tsp. (2.5 mL) kosher salt for the mushrooms + 1 tsp. (5 mL) for the egg mixture

1 tsp. (5 mL) freshly squeezed lemon juice

5 large eggs

1 egg yolk

2¼ cups (535 mL) chicken stock

3¼ cups (780 mL) 10% cream

⅛ heaping tsp. (0.5 mL) freshly ground white pepper

25 slices white bread, sandwich loaf shape with crusts on

8 oz. (225 g) full-fat ricotta, crumbled (or very thinly sliced brie)

Preheat the oven to 375°F (190°C).

Lightly rinse the four types of fresh mushrooms and drain. Cut the stalks off the Portobello, chanterelle, and shiitake mushrooms. Scrape the gills off the underside of the Portobello with a small spoon and cut into 1-inch (2.5-cm) chunks. Slice the button mushrooms and cut the shiitakes and chanterelles in quarters or halves, depending on size.

Drain the porcini mushrooms and pat dry. Mince and reserve.

Place the sliced leeks in a large bowl and fill with cold water. Within a few minutes, the dirt from the leeks will have settled to the bottom of the bowl. Drain the leeks and pat dry.

Melt the butter and 1 Tbsp. (15 mL) olive oil in a frying pan large enough to hold the mushrooms.

Add all the mushrooms except the porcinis and sauté over medium heat until the mushrooms have released all their liquid and are almost cooked. Add the garlic, thyme, ½ tsp. (2.5 mL) salt, and minced porcinis, and sauté another minute. Remove from heat and squeeze in lemon juice.

Slowly sauté the leeks over medium-low heat in the remaining 1½ Tbsp. (22.5 mL) olive oil for about 10 minutes or until the leeks are soft but not brown.

Crack the eggs into a bowl, with the egg yolk, and whisk together with the stock, cream, 1 tsp. (5 mL) salt, and pepper.

Cut the slices of bread in half diagonally and place 1 slightly overlapping layer in an 8- × 13- × 2-inch (20- × 33- × 5-cm), 12 cup (2.85 L) capacity casserole dish.

Spread half the leeks over the bread, then half the mushrooms.

Overlap another layer of bread, and layer the rest of the leeks and mushrooms. Top with the cheese.

Cut the remaining bread in 1-inch (2.5-cm) chunks and distribute over the cheese layer. Add more bread if necessary. The cheese should be barely visible.

Pour the egg-and-cream mixture over the strata, making sure to moisten the top layer. Cover tightly with plastic wrap, press down, and let stand for at least 30 minutes.

Remove wrap and bake for about 1 hour, or until the custard is set. Let the strata rest for 15 to 20 minutes before serving.

COOK'S TIPS

1. Scraping the gills from the Portobello mushroom will prevent the strata from turning an unattractive shade of brown.

2. Save the porcini water to use in soups and risotto. It can be frozen for up to 6 months.

Broccoli Purée with Lemon-Garlic Breadcrumbs

SERVES 4

Broccoli can be boiled, steamed, and roasted. It can be served hot, tossed with lemon butter, or cold in a salad, but my favourite way to prepare broccoli is as a purée. You can make it up to a day ahead if you have followed the method for retaining its colour. Reheat it over a bain marie (see page 42) until very warm or in the microwave.

2 tsp. (10 mL) olive oil
2 to 3 slices of fresh white bread ground into
  coarse breadcrumbs (see Cook's Tip)
zest of ⅓ lemon in long strands
2 large bunches broccoli
juice of ½ lemon

¼ tsp. (1.2 mL) grated garlic
6 to 8 Tbsp. (90 to 120 mL) extra-virgin
  olive oil
kosher salt and freshly ground white pepper
  to taste

Heat oil in a frying pan for 1 minute over medium heat. Add breadcrumbs and sauté until golden, about 5 minutes. Remove from the heat and toss in lemon zest.

Steam the broccoli until just cooked, about 4 to 5 minutes, and immediately plunge into cold water to retain the colour. When the broccoli is cool, drain, and pat very dry. Remove as much moisture as possible.

Purée the broccoli with half the lemon juice, the garlic, and 4 Tbsp. (60 mL) olive oil.

Slowly add more olive oil to reach a smooth consistency. Taste and season with salt, pepper, and more lemon juice if desired.

Top with toasted breadcrumbs and serve.

COOK'S TIP

Breadcrumbs are a staple in my kitchen. I take my fresh or stale bread, whirl it in the food processor, bag the crumbs, and freeze them until needed. Fresh bread should not be pulverized as long as stale bread or it will become gummy—fresh bread crumbs are larger and more irregular than their stale bread cousins.

Although broccoli is enjoyed worldwide today, its origins are in Italy. The vegetable made its way to France in the sixteenth century when the marriage of Catherine de Medici to Henry II opened up trade between the two countries. Broccoli was not grown in North America until well into the 1700s.

Desserts

Tropical Fruit Summer Pudding with Rum Custard   173

Antiguan Caramelized Bananas over Vanilla Ice Cream   175

Maple Ginger Crème Brulée with Candied Walnuts   176

Chocolate Bread Pudding with Coffee Crème Anglaise   178

Ginger Biscotti   181

Bread Bits for Kings   182

Apple and Orange Walnut Cake with Orange Calvados Glaze
or Orange Cream Cheese Frosting   184

Baby Cakes   187

Coconut Sorbet with Sautéed Mangoes and Patty's Oatmeal Shortbread   189

Plum, Cardamom and Hazelnut Crisp   191

Ice Cream Surprise Cake   192

"C is for cookie; that's good enough for me."
—Cookie Monster

Tropical Fruit Summer Pudding with Rum Custard

SERVES 8

Pineapple, papaya, and orange play a role in this exotic take on summer pudding. The beautiful seeds of the passion fruit (available almost year-round) are the crowning touch. You can make one large dessert in a loaf pan but I prefer small individual servings. The rum custard, flavoured with a hint of nutmeg, is thicker than a crème anglaise and adds a hint of decadence to this fruit-and-bread dessert.

12 ripe passion fruit (see Cook's Tips)
⅓ cup (80 mL) granulated sugar
⅔ cup (160 mL) water
2½ cups (600 mL) finely chopped fresh
 pineapple
1½ cups (360 mL) finely chopped fresh
 papaya

2 Tbsp. (30 mL) icing sugar
twelve ½-inch (1.2-cm) slices good quality
 white bread, crusts removed
2 oranges or blood oranges, peeled and
 segmented, pith removed (see Cook's Tips)
RUM CUSTARD (SEE PAGE 174)

Cut each passion fruit in half and scrape the seeds and pulp into a bowl with a small spoon. In a small saucepan, bring the granulated sugar and water to a boil. Remove from heat and mix in the passion fruit seeds and pulp.

In a separate bowl, add the pineapple and papaya. Toss with the icing sugar.

Line 8 small 2- × 4-inch (5- × 10-cm) loaf pans with plastic wrap, leaving enough overhang to cover the top. Cut the bread to fit the pans. It is imperative that the first layer of bread you lay down be in one piece as this will be the top of the pudding. Subsequent layers can be fitted together from odd sizes of bread if need be. Dip one side of each slice of bread in the passion fruit glaze and place, dipped-side down, on the bottom of each loaf pan. Follow with a layer of the pineapple-papaya mix and then top with 2 to 3 segments of orange per loaf tin. Repeat with the bread and fruit for a second layer. Finish with one last slice of bread, dipped-side up. Set aside the remaining passion fruit glaze for serving.

Cover the top of each loaf pan with the overhanging plastic wrap. Place some weights on the top of each pudding. Pie weights or small river stones work well. (For one large pudding, use soup cans.) Refrigerate for at least 24 hours.

Half an hour before serving, turn the puddings out onto plates and cover with the remaining passion fruit glaze, making sure to spread the seeds evenly over the top. Accompany with a few tablespoons of rum custard.

COOK'S TIPS

1. Cut the top and bottom off the oranges. Stand on one end and, using a sharp knife, slice down the sides of the orange to remove the peel, the pith, and the stringy outside membrane of each segment. Continue around the whole orange. Slice between the segments of each orange to release the flesh from its membrane.

2. Buy your passion fruits several days ahead of preparing and keep at room temperature until the skins are wrinkled. This will ensure that the passion fruit is ripe and sweet.

Rum Custard

2 cups (475 mL) homogenized milk
pinch ground nutmeg
scraped seeds from ½ vanilla bean or ½ tsp.
   (2.5 mL) vanilla essence
6 large egg yolks
¼ cup (60 mL) granulated sugar
1 Tbsp. + 1 tsp. (20 mL) dark rum

Pour the milk into a saucepan large enough to hold all the ingredients. Over medium-low heat, scald the milk (see Cook's Tip below). Immediately remove from the heat and add the grated nutmeg and vanilla. Let sit for 15 minutes.

Whisk the egg yolks and sugar until well blended, about 30 seconds, in a bowl large enough to hold the scalded milk.

Meanwhile, place another similar-sized bowl in a larger bowl filled with ice.

Slowly, to prevent the eggs from scrambling, drizzle the scalded milk into the eggs, whisking constantly. Pour the mixture back into the saucepan, return to medium-low heat, and stir continuously for about 15 minutes with a wooden spoon until the custard has the consistency of lightly whipped cream.

Immediately pour the custard into the bowl surrounded by ice and stir in the rum. When the custard reaches room temperature, press plastic wrap on the surface to prevent a skin from forming. Refrigerate until half an hour before serving.

COOK'S TIP

Scald milk by heating it in a heavy bottomed saucepan until tiny bubbles form around the inside edges of the pot. Remove the pot from the heat and cover. This allows the milk to become infused with flavours, in this case vanilla and nutmeg.

Antiguan Caramelized Bananas over Vanilla Ice Cream

SERVES 4

You will find a rendition of this lovely dessert when visiting most Caribbean Islands. Each cook personalizes it to make it his or her own. At home, we call this "Mrs. Pellegrino's Bananas" as we first tasted it at her house in Antigua. If, by any chance, you have any bananas left over, serve the next day over French toast.

3 large bananas
½ cup (120 mL) packed brown sugar
⅓ cup (80 mL) water
⅛ tsp. (0.5 mL) ground nutmeg
½ tsp. (2.5 mL) ground cinnamon
1 Tbsp. (15 mL) freshly squeezed lime juice
1 Tbsp. (15 mL) dark rum
good quality vanilla ice cream

Cut the bananas in half lengthwise and then widthwise, so that you end up with 12 banana pieces.

Put the sugar and water in a frying pan large enough to hold all the bananas in one layer. Heat over medium-high until the sugar melts. Add the nutmeg, cinnamon, and lime juice; simmer for 1 to 3 minutes or until the sauce thickens slightly. Reduce the heat if the sauce starts to boil.

Add the bananas. Cover with sauce and simmer for just 2 minutes more. The bananas should retain their shape and not be mushy.

Meanwhile, heat the rum in a small saucepan over medium heat. Remove the bananas from the heat. Carefully pour the rum over the bananas and light with a match. The alcohol will flame and then die out.

Serve warm bananas and sauce over vanilla ice cream.

COOK'S TIP

Hyacinth Anderson, who is from Jamaica, makes this quick-and-easy dessert in the oven. Preheat the oven to 375°F (190°C). Lay the cut bananas in a baking dish. Mix the sugar, water, and lime juice together and pour over the bananas. Sprinkle with the nutmeg and cinnamon. Bake, uncovered, for 10 minutes. Spoon the sauce over the bananas and bake for another 15 minutes, making sure the sugar syrup doesn't burn and the bananas don't turn mushy. Remove from the oven and flambé with the rum. To be very authentic, serve with coconut cream, evaporated milk, or vanilla ice cream.

Maple Ginger Crème Brûlée with Candied Walnuts

MAKES 8 SERVINGS

Maple syrup and fresh ginger make wonderful companions when mixed with eggs, cream, and a little sugar. If ginger is a passion, add an extra teaspoon (5 mL). The candied walnuts are also delicious eaten on their own or can be used to decorate the Apple and Orange Walnut Cake (see page 184). If you prefer a traditional crème brûlée, leave out the ginger and substitute ¼ cup (60 mL) granulated sugar for the maple syrup.

1 vanilla bean, split lengthwise
5 cups (1.2 L) 18% cream
9 large egg yolks
pinch of kosher salt
¼ cup + 1 Tbsp. (75 mL) maple syrup
2 tsp. (10 mL) grated fresh ginger
½ to ¾ cup (120 to 180 mL) fine sugar, (see
   Cook's Tip page 33)

CANDIED WALNUTS
16 walnut halves
2 Tbsp. (30 mL) maple syrup
1½ tsp. (7.5 mL) minced fresh lemon thyme
   (optional)

Preheat the oven to 325°F (165°C).

Split the vanilla bean lengthwise and, with the blunt side of a paring knife, scrape the seeds into the cream.

In a medium saucepan over medium-low heat, add the cream and the scraped pod. Scald the cream-vanilla pod mixture (see Cook's Tip 3, page 174). Immediately remove from heat and set aside until lukewarm. Once lukewarm, remove the vanilla bean pod and discard.

In a large bowl, whisk the egg yolks together with the salt, maple syrup, and ginger until well combined.

Slowly, to prevent the eggs from scrambling, stir the lukewarm cream into the egg mixture. Skim off any bubbles that have formed.

Ladle the cream-and-egg mixture into eight ¾-cup (180-mL) ramekins or small gratin dishes, or for one large custard, into a 6-cup (1.5-L) oven-proof dish. When ladling, make sure to get vanilla bean seeds into each ramekin or dish. (You may have a little custard left over.) Cover each ramekin with tin foil.

Place the foil-covered ramekins into a roasting pan with high sides and put in the oven. Pour warm water into the roasting pan until the water is halfway up the sides of the ramekins. Bake for 30 to 55 minutes depending on the size and depth of dish you have used. When done, a skewer plunged into the center of a custard should come out clean. The custard will be slightly wobbly in the middle.

Cool the dishes on a counter for about an hour, before refrigerating for at least 2 hours. The Crème Brûlée can be made 24 hours ahead and refrigerated until it is time to brûlée the tops (see Cook's Tip 1). An hour before serving, remove from the refrigerator and generously sprinkle the tops of each custard with sugar. Brûlée the tops with a propane torch or place the ramekins under a very hot broiler (see Cook's Tip 2) until the sugar is melted and turns golden brown. Do not return to the refrigerator. Your brûléed top will "melt."

Before serving, top each dish with two candied walnuts.

FOR THE CANDIED WALNUTS

Preheat the oven to 350°F (175°C).

Warm a frying pan slightly over medium heat. Add the walnuts in one layer and cook for about one minute, shaking the pan continuously.

Add the maple syrup and cook for 15 to 20 seconds more or until the syrup disappears, making sure not to burn the nuts. Toss in the lemon thyme. Transfer the walnuts onto a baking sheet, in one layer, and bake for 5 to 7 minutes, taking care not to burn the nuts. Remove the candied walnuts from the pan immediately and cool.

COOK'S TIPS

1. It is important that the custards are cold before you start the brûléeing process. If they are not, the beautiful, hard surface will turn to liquid sugar within an hour or so.

2. When using a hot broiler to caramelize the sugar, place the ramekins in a larger oven-proof dish half filled with ice water. This will prevent the custard from overheating.

Chocolate Bread Pudding with Coffee Crème Anglaise

SERVES 10 TO 12

Bread pudding can be made with a myriad of fruits and a variety of flavours but when you add chocolate to the equation it ups the ante. And now that chocolate has been found to contain antioxidants there's even more reason to enjoy this decadent dessert. The little bit of strong coffee in the Crème Anglaise cuts the richness of the chocolate, eggs, and cream.

8 oz. (225 g) semi-sweet chocolate plus 1 oz. (28 g) for drizzling
4 cups (950 mL) homogenized milk
3½ cups (840 mL) 35% cream
1 vanilla bean, split horizontally
4 cloves
8 large eggs
1 cup (240 mL) granulated sugar
pinch of kosher salt

2 Tbsp. (30 mL) Tia Maria or Kahlua
4 Tbsp. (60 mL) cocoa powder
3 Tbsp. (45 mL) strong coffee
forty ¼-inch (6-mm) slices pain au lait, brioche, or good quality white sandwich loaf, crusts removed
1 tsp. (5 mL) unsalted butter, to grease the casserole dish
COFFEE CRÈME ANGLAISE (SEE PAGE 180)

Preheat the oven to 350°F (175°C).

Chop the 8 oz. (225 g) of chocolate into small pieces and melt (see Cook's Tip). Let cool to lukewarm. Meanwhile, chop the 1 oz. (28 g) of chocolate and set aside. (You will melt it before serving the pudding.)

Pour the milk and cream into a large saucepan. Scrape the seeds from the vanilla bean with the blunt side of a paring knife and add the seeds, scraped pods, and cloves to the milk and cream. Scald (see Cook's Tip 3, page 174) the milk mixture in a heavy bottomed saucepan over medium-high heat. Immediately remove from the heat, cover to keep warm, and let infuse for 30 minutes.

In a medium bowl, whisk the eggs with the sugar and a pinch of salt; add the liqueur and continue whisking.

Remove the cloves and vanilla pod from the milk and discard. Whisk in the cocoa and then stir in the coffee and melted chocolate.

Slowly drizzle the chocolate–coffee mixture into the egg mixture, whisking continuously.

Lay pieces of bread on the bottom of a greased 9- × 13- × 2-inch (23- × 33- × 5-cm) oven-proof casserole dish. Don't overlap the bread but make sure the bottom of the dish is completely covered.

Drizzle 2½ cups (600 mL) of the chocolate-coffee-egg mixture over the layer of bread. Add another layer of bread and another 2 cups (475 mL) of the chocolate-coffee-egg mixture, making sure all the bread is soaked.

Cut 3-inch (7.5-cm) circles from the last pieces of bread and overlap them to form the top layer of the pudding. Gently pour all but 2 cups (475 mL) of the chocolate-coffee-egg mixture over the top of the bread.

Press down the pudding using your hands and cover tightly with plastic wrap. Let sit for at least 1½ hours, occasionally pressing down on top of the plastic wrap to completely saturate the bread. If you wish to assemble the pudding earlier in the day, refrigerate it, and bring back to room temperature before baking.

Preheat the oven to 350°F (175°C).

Drizzle on ½ cup (120 mL) of the chocolate-coffee-egg mixture before placing the casserole dish in a deep baking pan with a lip. Fill the baking pan with warm water half way up the side of the casserole dish and bake for 15 minutes before drizzling on the remaining chocolate mixture. Bake for about another 40 minutes or until the custard is set and no liquid is visible.

Melt the remaining 1 oz. (28 g) chocolate.

Remove the pudding from the oven and let cool for at least 20 to 25 minutes before cutting. Drizzle with as much melted chocolate as you like. Serve warm with Coffee Crème Anglaise. The Coffee Crème Anglaise should be cool or at room temperature, but not cold.

COOK'S TIP

When melting chocolate in the microwave, coarsely chop it before microwaving on high in 20-second intervals, stirring in between. When only a few soft lumps remain, remove the chocolate from the microwave and stir until those lumps melt. To melt chocolate on the stove, simply use a double boiler or a metal bowl placed over a saucepan, making sure the water doesn't touch the bottom of the bowl. Stir occasionally until the chocolate is melted.

Coffee Crème Anglaise

For those who want an exceptionally smooth crème anglaise, taking an additional step that uses a fine sieve will make it so. Just pour the hot crème anglaise through the sieve to remove any small lumps or curds that have formed during the cooking process. Crème anglaise has the consistency of thick pouring cream.

1¾ cups (420 mL) homogenized milk
1 tsp. (5 mL) pure vanilla extract or 1 vanilla
   bean, split lengthwise
3 Tbsp. (45 mL) strong coffee (¼ cup/60 mL)
   dark roasted ground coffee brewed with
   ¾ cup/180 mL hot water)
4 large egg yolks
½ cup (120 mL) granulated sugar

Pour the milk into a medium saucepan. If you are using the vanilla bean, scrape out the seeds and add the seeds and scraped pod to the milk. Scald the milk (see Cook's Tip, page 174) over medium-low heat. Immediately remove from the heat. Add the coffee and the vanilla extract (if you haven't added the vanilla seeds and pod) to the milk. Let sit for 15 minutes.

In a medium bowl, whisk the eggs and sugar together.

Meanwhile, place another medium bowl in a larger bowl filled with ice.

Slowly whisk the warm vanilla-flavoured milk into the egg mixture. Transfer the milk-and-egg mixture to the saucepan and return to medium-low heat.

Stir continuously with a wooden spoon for 7 to 9 minutes or until the mixture has thickened just slightly. The crème anglaise is ready when you can lift the spoon out, draw your finger across the back of the spoon, and the line doesn't fill in.

Remove the vanilla pod, if using, from custard and discard. Pour the custard into the bowl surrounded by ice. When the custard reaches room temperature, press plastic wrap onto the surface to prevent a skin from forming. Refrigerate until half an hour before serving.

Ginger Biscotti

MAKES ABOUT 30 TO 40 COOKIES

Enoch Grey used to make our biscotti when we first opened ACE over ten years ago. He made many different kinds but this ginger delight was the most popular. Biscotti will keep for a couple of weeks if stored in a covered container, so you may want to make a double batch.

3 cups (720 mL) unbleached all-purpose flour
1½ cups + 2 Tbsp. (390 mL) granulated sugar
1¼ tsp. (6.2 mL) baking powder
1 heaping tsp. (5 mL) kosher salt
1½ Tbsp. (22.5 mL) ground ginger
½ tsp. (2.5 mL) ground cinnamon
½ tsp. (2.5 mL) ground nutmeg

1 cup (240 mL) finely chopped crystallized
  ginger
½ cup + 2 Tbsp. (150 mL) vegetable oil
4 large eggs
1 egg mixed with 1 Tbsp. (15 mL)
  homogenized milk, for glazing

Preheat the oven to 325°F (165°C).

In a standing mixer, using a dough hook, combine all the dry ingredients including the crystallized ginger at "stir" speed.

In a separate bowl, whisk the vegetable oil and the eggs together until well combined.

Slowly combine the egg mixture with the dry ingredients in the standing mixer at "stir" speed until a dough forms into a smooth ball. If it doesn't form into a ball, remove from the bowl and form into a ball by hand using a sprinkling of flour. The dough will be quite sticky and is easier to handle with wet hands, so keep a bowl of water nearby to occasionally moisten your hands. Separate the dough into 3 equal pieces; form all into logs equal in width and length.

Place the logs on 1 or 2 greased and floured baking sheets, leaving room to spread. Brush with egg wash and bake for 40 to 50 minutes on the middle rack, turning the rack once, halfway through the baking time. When done, the biscotti should be firm when pressed with a fingertip.

Remove from oven and let cool completely.

When cool, cut the biscotti diagonally into ½-inch (1.2-cm) slices, using a serrated knife so as not to crumble or break the biscotti into pieces.

Place flat side down on a baking sheet and bake for an additional 10 to 14 minutes at 325°F (165°C) or until light golden. Allow to cool completely before serving.

COOK'S TIP

A flexible plastic dough scraper will be helpful if you are having trouble removing the raw dough from the mixing bowl.

Bread Bits for Kings

SERVES 6 TO 8

This is my friend Nalini's family recipe for an Indian-style bread pudding. Like most Indian desserts, it is very sweet—consequently, small portions are in order. The suggestion of cardamom and rose water can be picked up in the finished dish. Nalini serves this after an Indian meal with a bowl of fresh fruit. You could have it as dessert after the Rosemary Skewered Grilled Shrimp on Summer Vegetables (see page 155) or the Orange Steamed Mussels with Tomatoes and Breadcrumbs (see page 152).

6 slices white sliced bread, sandwich-loaf shaped
1 cup (240 mL) granulated sugar
2 cups (475 mL) water
1½ cups (360 mL) homogenized milk
4 green cardamom pods (see Cook's Tip)
1 to 2 cups (240 to 475 mL) fresh safflower or canola oil

1 tsp. (5 mL) rose water
¼ cup (60 mL) chopped pistachios
¼ cup (60 mL) flaked almonds
fresh unsprayed pink rose petals (optional for decoration)
good quality vanilla ice cream

Cut the crusts off the bread and then cut each slice into 4 triangles; set aside.

In a small saucepan, mix together the sugar and water and cook over low heat, stirring occasionally, about 45 minutes or until it has formed a light golden syrup. Remove the pan from the heat.

Meanwhile, in a separate medium saucepan, bring the milk to a boil over medium heat with the lid on. Take the lid off and immediately turn the heat to medium-low. Gently simmer for 35 to 45 minutes, or until the liquid is reduced to just over ½ cup (120 mL), stirring almost constantly to prevent it from clinging to the sides of the pot and burning. It will be a light yellow colour and coat the back of a spoon. Remove from heat and set aside.

Split open the cardamom pods and grind the tiny seeds in a spice grinder or a mortar and pestle.

Heat the oil in a small saucepan over medium to high heat until hot. A thermometer, when inserted, should read 350° to 360°F (175° to 182°C). Drop in pieces of bread in batches of 4 and cook for a few seconds on each side or until golden and crisp on the outside but still soft in the middle. Drain on paper towels.

Once all the bread is fried, quickly dip each slice in the sugar syrup and arrange, slightly overlapping, on a platter. Sprinkle with rose water, pistachios, and almonds. Dust ⅛ to ¼ tsp. (0.5 to 1.2 mL) freshly ground cardamom seeds over top. Sprinkle with rose petals.

Drizzle the thickened milk over the dessert just before serving with vanilla ice cream.

COOK'S TIP

Store-brought ground cardamom powder has a completely different taste from the seeds of green cardamom pods, as do the seeds from black cardamom pods. Don't use the spice unless you can find the green pods.

Apple and Orange Walnut Cake with Orange Calvados Glaze or Orange Cream Cheese Frosting

MAKES ONE (8½-INCH/21.2-CM) CAKE

Breadcrumbs and ground walnuts take the place of flour in this moist, dense confection. The grated apple helps the cake to stay fresh for 4 to 5 days. I've given you two ideas for topping—an Orange Cream Cheese Frosting, sure to please the kids in the group, and an Orange Calvados Glaze. It is also very good served plain with just a dusting of icing sugar.

1 cup (240 mL) fine sugar (see Cook's Tip, page 33)
1⅓ cups (320 mL) very fine dried bread-crumbs
1 cup (240 mL) ground walnuts, approximately 2 cups (475 mL) walnut halves (See Cook's Tip, page 185)
1 Tbsp. (15 mL) baking powder
½ cup (120 mL) cubed, cold unsalted butter
1 tsp. (5 mL) grated orange zest
1 peeled and coarsely grated Granny Smith apple, about 1 scant cup (240 mL)
6 egg whites
Orange Cream Cheese Frosting or 3 to 4 Tbsp. (45 to 60 mL) Orange Calvados Glaze

ORANGE CALVADOS GLAZE
½ cup (120 mL) icing sugar
1 Tbsp. (15 mL) freshly squeezed orange juice
1 Tbsp. (15 mL) freshly squeezed lemon juice
2½ tsp (12.5 mL) Calvados liqueur

ORANGE CREAM CHEESE FROSTING
6 Tbsp. (90 mL) softened unsalted butter
½ lb. (225 g) cream cheese, cut into ½- to 1-inch (1.2- to 2.5-cm) chunks
1 tsp. (5 mL) pure vanilla extract
1 tsp. (5 mL) grated orange zest
pinch kosher salt
1 cup (240 mL) icing sugar

Preheat the oven to 350°F (175°C).

Lightly grease an 8½- to 9-inch (21.2- to 23-cm) springform pan. Cut a piece of parchment paper to fit the bottom of the pan. Put parchment paper in the pan and grease it as well.

Place the sugar, breadcrumbs, ground walnuts, and baking powder in a food processor and pulse to combine.

Add the cubed butter to the breadcrumb mixture and continue pulsing until well combined and the mixture has the consistency of moist brown sugar.

Transfer to a mixing bowl and stir in the orange zest and the apple.

In a separate large mixing bowl, beat the egg whites until very stiff peaks form.

Fold 1 cup (240 mL) of the beaten egg whites into the breadcrumb mixture to lighten it up. Gently fold in the remaining egg whites in two additions.

Pour the batter into the prepared springform pan and bake for 50 to 60 minutes or until a skewer, inserted into the middle of the cake, comes out glistening but clean.

Remove from the oven onto a cooling rack and let rest for at least 10 minutes. Run a knife around the edges of the pan and remove the sides. Let the cake finish cooling before removing the bottom of the pan and parchment paper. Transfer to a serving plate. Frost with the icing or drizzle with 3 to 4 Tbsp. (45 to 60 mL) warm glaze.

ORANGE CALVADOS GLAZE

Spoon the sugar into a small mixing bowl and whisk in the two juices. Transfer to a saucepan and quickly bring to a boil over high heat. Remove from heat and spoon over the cake while still hot; discard any remaining glaze.

ORANGE CREAM CHEESE FROSTING

Cream the butter with an electric mixer or standing mixer in a mixing bowl large enough to hold all the ingredients. Add the cream cheese, vanilla, orange zest, and salt; continue mixing until just combined. Gently mix in half the icing sugar, and, when just combined, mix in the remaining half. Spread over the sides and top of the cooled cake and refrigerate until ready to serve.

COOK'S TIPS

1. Grind the walnuts with ¼ cup (60 mL) of the 1 cup (240 mL) of sugar called for in the recipe. The ground nuts will stay fluffy and not disintegrate into a paste.

2. Once you have opened a package of shelled walnuts, wrap what you haven't used and store in the refrigerator or freezer. Walnuts will keep in the refrigerator for up to 6 months and in the freezer for almost a year.

Walnuts contain a heart-healthy omega-3 fatty acid, which doctors think may help prevent heart attacks. They also contain polyunsaturated and monounsaturated oils, which are thought to lower blood cholesterol.

Baby Cakes

MAKES 6 BABY CAKES OR 1 (8½- × 4½-INCH/21.2- × 11.2-CM) LOAF

We used to make these exquisite little cakes in the café. Baby cakes are at their best when baked in 3-inch (7.5-cm) high timbale cups, which produce individual portions with tall, straight sides. Good kitchenware stores carry them. You can also bake the dough in a loaf pan. This is a slow-rising sticky dough which produces a dense cake that will stay fresh for 3 to 4 days if tightly wrapped at room temperature. These are delicious on their own or served with fresh berries and whipped cream.

7¼ oz. (208 g) almond paste, not marzipan (see Cook's Tip)
¾ cup (180 mL) granulated sugar
⅔ cup (160 mL) cold unsalted butter, cut into cubes
3 extra-large eggs

¼ tsp. (1.2 mL) orange oil or orange extract
⅔ cup (160 mL) all-purpose flour
¼ tsp. (1.2 mL) baking powder
¼ tsp. (1.2 mL) kosher salt
1 oz. (28 g) candied ginger, finely chopped
unsalted butter, to grease timbale cups

Preheat the oven to 325°F (165°C).

Break the almond paste into walnut-sized chunks and place in a food processor with the white sugar. Process until the almond paste has broken up and amalgamated with the sugar into a thick paste.

Add the cold cubed butter and process until the mixture is light and creamy.

In a small bowl, lightly whisk together the eggs and the orange oil. Slowly add the eggs to the almond paste mixture, while processing.

Add the dry ingredients, including the ginger, to the batter and pulse until just combined.

Pour the batter into greased and floured timbale cups or large muffin cups or into a well-greased and floured 8½- × 4½-inch (21.2- × 11.2-cm) loaf pan.

Bake until golden: 25 minutes for the timbale cups, 55 to 65 minutes for the loaf pan, or until a cake tester inserted into the middle comes out clean. Cool in the pan for about 15 minutes before turning out onto a baking rack.

COOK'S TIP

Almond paste contains fewer additives and less sugar than marzipan and is meant to be used in baking. It is available at specialty food and baking shops, and for order over the internet.

A timbale cup is a small cylindrical mould used to shape sweet or savoury custards and rice mixtures. They are available at commercial or high-end cookware shops. You can use a muffin tin (the cakes will bake in about 20 to 25 minutes) but the look won't be as pleasing.

Patty's Oatmeal Shortbread p. 190

Coconut Sorbet with Sautéed Mangoes and Patty's Oatmeal Shortbread

MAKES ABOUT 6 CUPS (1.5 L) OF SORBET

Coconut sorbet is light and fresh, and is a perfect foil for warm mango slices sautéed in butter, sugar, lime, and rum. You will be transported to sunny climates with your first bite. A couple of my friend Patty's Oatmeal Shortbread (see page 190) are a perfect addition to an already scrumptious dessert.

½ cup (120 mL) granulated sugar
½ cup (120 mL) water
3 ¾ cups (796 mL) chilled coconut milk (2 cans) (see Cook's Tip)
¼ cup (60 mL) light corn syrup
1 Tbsp. (15 mL) white rum

SAUTÉED MANGOES (SERVES 6)
3 Tbsp. (45 mL) unsalted butter
grated zest of one organic lime
juice of two limes
2 Tbsp. (30 mL) packed brown sugar
2 Tbsp. (30 mL) dark rum
3 ripe mangoes, peeled, pitted and thinly sliced, ⅜-inch (9.5-mm) thick

In a small saucepan, bring the sugar and water to a boil over high heat. When all the sugar is dissolved, remove from heat and cool.

Pour chilled coconut milk into a large bowl and whisk in the corn syrup until thoroughly mixed.

Stir in ½ cup (120 mL) sugar syrup and the rum. Pour into an ice cream maker and freeze according to the manufacturer's instructions.

FOR SAUTÉED MANGOES

Melt the butter over medium-high heat in a frying pan. Add the lime zest, lime juice, sugar, and rum. Stir until the sugar dissolves. Add the mango slices, and simmer until just heated through. (The mango slices will fall apart if over-cooked.)

COOK'S TIP

Buy premium canned coconut milk. When testing this recipe I found there to be a huge difference in the quality of the brands available.

Mangoes were originally native to India and can be eaten at any stage of ripeness. In India, as well as in Malaysia and Thailand, under-ripe green mangoes are commonly used in chutneys and in many of the same ways tart green apples are used in the West.

Patty's Oatmeal Shortbread

MAKES ABOUT 3 DOZEN COOKIES

1 cup (240 mL) softened unsalted butter
1 cup (240 mL) lightly-packed light brown
   sugar
1½ cups (360 mL) sifted cake flour
¾ tsp. (4 mL) kosher salt
½ tsp. baking soda
2 cups (475 mL) quick-cooking oatmeal (not
   instant)

Preheat the oven to 350°F (175°C).

In a medium bowl, mix together the butter and the sugar with a hand mixer or using the paddle on a standing mixer.

In a separate bowl, whisk together the flour, salt, and baking soda. Mix 1 cup (240 mL) flour into the butter and sugar, followed by 1 cup (240 mL) oatmeal. Repeat with the remaining flour and oatmeal.

Drop hard-packed heaping tablespoons (15 mL) of dough on an ungreased cookie sheet. A one tablespoon ice cream scoop works well too. Gently press each cookie with a lightly-floured fork to make 1½-inch (3.8-cm) circles. The cookies should be lightly marked with the tines of the fork and flat on top.

Bake for 10 to 13 minutes or until pale golden, and cool on a rack.

Shortbread, traditionally round with notched edges to signify the sun's rays, was originally served at Christmas and Hogmanay (Scottish New Year's Eve).

Plum, Cardamom and Hazelnut Crisp

SERVES 8 TO 10

Hazelnuts, thought by the Ancient Chinese to be a sacred food sent to us from heaven, add a rich flavour and texture to the crisp topping. I've used fresh breadcrumbs and cubed bread instead of flour as well as hints of orange, cardamom, and white pepper mixed in with the plums. This crisp would be perfect served after the Stuffed Pork Chops with Pomegranate Maple-Glaze (see page 143) or Roasted Chicken on a Bed of Potatoes, Mushrooms and Shallots (see page 144).

12 to 14 large ripe but firm prune plums, seeded and cut in halves or quarters, depending on size
4 large ripe but firm Angelino, Santa Rosa, or Friar plums, seeded and cut in eighths
½ tsp. (2.5 mL) packed orange zest
2 Tbsp. (30 mL) packed brown sugar
¼ tsp. (1.2 mL) ground cardamom
⅛ tsp. (0.5 mL) freshly ground white pepper
½ heaping tsp. (2.5 mL) cornstarch

12 ½-inch (1.2-cm) slices fresh crustless white bread
4 ½-inch (1.2-cm) slices fresh crustless bread cut into ½-inch (1.2-cm) cubes
¼ cup (60 mL) plus 2 Tbsp. (30 mL) packed brown sugar
¼ heaping cup (60 mL) hazelnuts, roughly chopped
¾ cup (180 mL) cold unsalted butter, cut into ¼-inch (6-mm) cubes

Preheat the oven to 375°F (190°C).

In a large bowl, toss the plums with the orange zest, 2 Tbsp. (30 mL) brown sugar, cardamom, white pepper, and cornstarch. You should have about 9 to 10 cups (2.1 to 2.4 L) of filling. Transfer to a 8- × 12-inch (20- × 30-cm) oven-proof dish with a 2- to 2½-inch (5- × 56-mm) lip. The plums should be almost level with the top of the dish.

Pulse the 12 slices of bread in a food processor until crumbs are about ⅛-inch (3-mm) in size. Toss the breadcrumbs, cubed bread, remaining brown sugar, hazelnuts, and butter in a large bowl and spoon the mixture over the plums.

Bake for 35 to 40 minutes until the top is dark golden brown. Serve warm, not hot, with a scoop of good quality vanilla ice cream.

COOK'S TIP
A sturdy melon baller will help you remove stubborn prune pits.

"What is more mortifying than to feel that you have missed the plum for want of courage to shake the tree?"

—Logan Pearsall Smith

Ice Cream Surprise Cake

SERVES 6 TO 8

My friends and I used to whip up this "surprise" as a special treat for our kids when they spent the afternoon playing together. Children aren't the only ones who will love this dome of ice cream encasing fresh berries mixed with ladyfingers. When I'm making this for adults, I add Chambord, a raspberry liqueur, to the mix. Although the ice cream covering can be molded the day before, the filling can't be frozen for much more than 2 to 4 hours. If it is frozen too long, you will end up with a frozen block of berries that will be impossible to cut through.

4¼ cups (1L) slightly softened good quality vanilla ice cream
1½ cup (360 mL) raspberries
1½ cups (360 mL) blueberries
1⅓ cups (320 mL) ¼-inch (6-mm) finely crumbled ladyfingers

2 Tbsp. (30 mL) Chambord or framboise liqueur (optional)
1 cup (240 mL) whipping cream
1½ tsp. (7.5 mL) granulated sugar
½ tsp. (2.5 mL) pure vanilla extract

Line a 9-inch (23-cm), 8 cup (2 L) glass mixing bowl with plastic wrap and cover the inside with a 1-inch (2.5-cm) layer of vanilla ice cream. Freeze until hardened for 1½ hours to overnight.

Wash and gently dry the berries. Mix with the ladyfinger crumbs and liqueur, if using, and gently spoon into the cavity of the molded frozen ice cream.

Whip the cream with the sugar and vanilla until stiff peaks form. Using a spatula, spread on top of the berries and to the edges of the molded ice cream to form what will be the bottom "crust" of the cake.

Freeze, covered, for 2 to 4 hours or until the whipped cream has hardened.

Plunge a cake tester or skewer into the "cake" after 2 hours to test how quickly the centre is freezing. The tester should be able to plunge through the centre with a touch of resistance. If it feels soft, freeze for another ½ hour and test again.

Turn the cake onto a large plate just before serving and remove the bowl and plastic wrap. Garnish with fresh berries and mint leaves and serve immediately. To make for easier slicing, dip a sharp knife into a mug of hot water and wipe dry before cutting each slice.

COOK'S TIP

Everyone's freezer reads differently depending on how full it is and how the temperature is set. After you have made this cake once, you will be better able to gauge the correct timing.

Ice cream can be traced as far back as the fourth century B.C. One of the earliest recorded references is of the Roman Emperor Nero, who ordered ice to be brought down from the mountains to be combined with fruit. In the seventh century, China's Emperor Tan would come closer to making modern ice cream by creating milk and ice mixtures. It is believed that Marco Polo brought recipes to Italy from the Orient, creating a rage for ice cream throughout Europe.

Glossary and Baker's Lingo

active dry yeast or traditional yeast: The yeast most commonly found in the average kitchen. It is very potent and keeps for a relatively long time, up to a year sealed in its package, and a few months once opened, or longer if stored in the refrigerator. It needs to be rehydrated in lukewarm water before being added to a recipe.

all-purpose flour: Flour whose protein content falls between those of soft and hard flour and can be substituted for either, although the results won't be quite as pleasing as with the flour specifically suited for that purpose. When baking bread, hard flour should be used. (See hard flour)

ascorbic acid: Another name for vitamin C. Bakers sometimes add minute amounts to the dough to prevent it from collapsing.

autolyse: A resting period for dough, prior to the addition of salt, yeast, or pre-ferment, during which the flour can hydrate and the gluten can develop, smoothing the dough. The salt tightens the gluten, and the leaveners—the yeast or pre-ferment—acidify the dough, inhibiting hydration.

baguette: A long, relatively thin loaf of bread, developed in France.

bain marie: The French term for a double boiler or water bath.

banneton: A woven basket lined with raw linen cloth. When sprinkled with flour, it is used to rise boule-shaped pieces of dough.

bâtard: A shape similar to the baguette, but shorter and fatter.

benching: (See resting)

biga: An Italian pre-ferment, made of flour, water, and yeast, which is quite stiff. It can be fermented in a cool environment for up to 18 hours.

boule: A round bread, proofed upside-down in a basket (if it is a wet dough) designed to give it its shape.

butter: Most professional recipes, and the ones in this book, base their butter measurements on unsalted (or sweet) stick butter. The use of any other type of butter will result in a different end product unless other adjustments are made.

compressed yeast: The most active of the baking yeasts, preferred by most professional bakers. It should be stored in the refrigerator, tightly wrapped. If using it in a recipe that calls for active dry yeast, multiply the weight of active dry yeast called for by about two and a half, and simply crumble that amount of compressed yeast directly into the dough— no need to rehydrate.

couche: A heavy, raw-linen cloth that shaped breads, especially baguettes, can proof inside without forming a crust. The fabric is quite stiff and naturally non-stick, helping breads keep their shape as they rise.

crumb: The interior of the bread, especially with reference to the texture.

crust: The outside of a loaf of bread. In an artisan bread, color is valued as well as crispness. A dark crust indicates good caramelization, which will have added some of its flavour to the bread.

fermentation: The professional baker's term for the first rising of a dough, and any subsequent rising before it reaches its final shape.

ficelle: Like a baguette, but very thin, almost like a length of thick rope—about 1½ inches (3.8 cm) in diameter.

folding: This process is called for by many recipes when combining a light and a heavy mixture (for example, beaten egg whites into a batter) without destroying the delicacy of the lighter one. There are two methods. One, pour all of the lighter mixture onto the heavier one, use a spatula to drag the heavy mixture across the bottom and over the top of the lighter one, and continue—turning the bowl as you go—until the two mixtures combine. The second method is slightly different. Thoroughly mix a third of the lighter mixture into the heavier one as described above. The rest of the lighter mixture can be gently dragged through the heavier one until completely mixed. Folding a lighter mixture into a heavier one is easier than the other way around.

gluten: The protein formed when flour containing relatively high amounts of glutenin and gliadin is moistened. Gluten is what allows dough to keep its shape as it rises, preventing the air bubbles formed by the rising agent from collapsing.

hard flour: Flour milled from specific wheats with a relatively high protein content that turns into gluten when moistened. It is well suited to bread making.

hearth: The stone baking surface of a baker's oven.

instant yeast: Compared to active dry yeast, instant yeast has a much higher surface area relative to the size of its grains, so it absorbs moisture much more easily and doesn't need to be rehydrated in advance. It can take up to 20 minutes to activate, so you may want to add it to bread dough sooner than a recipe suggests, maybe before a short autolyse.

intermediate proofing: (See resting)

iodized salt: Salt with iodine added to combat hypothyroidism, a condition often caused by a dietary lack of iodine. But a diet too high in iodine is not healthy either, so if you get iodine from other sources it is best to use non-iodized salt.

kosher salt: Far less regular in shape than table salt, its crystals often form hollow, four-sided pyramids. It dissolves more quickly than table salt, but because of its irregular shape it has a higher air content. If you measure by volume, you must use considerably more kosher salt to get the same effect as with table salt. That's why it is always better to measure salt by weight, or be flexible in following recipes.

lame: The tool bakers use to slash the tops of their breads. It is usually a razor blade mounted on a wooden or plastic handle. A very sharp knife or scalpel can also be used.

marinate: To soak meat or seafood in a specially prepared liquid. The flavour acquired from marinating is only one of the results. An acidic marinade will tenderize even the toughest meat. Leaving fish to stand in lemon or lime juice has the same effect as cooking it, and an oily marinade will make lean or dry meat more appetizing by adding some flavour-carrying fat. Today the term is also used for a mixture of dry ingredients that are rubbed into meat, poultry, or fish.

non-wheat flours: Flours made from grains other than wheat, such as rye, semolina, or oats. These don't contain the proteins that allow a dough to rise, and so must be combined with wheat flour unless you want a very dense final product.

oils: Aside from flavour, two factors help determine what kind of oil to use in a recipe: the predominant type of fat in the oil, and the smoke point. Of the common vegetable oils used in cooking, coconut and palm oil are highest in saturated fat, safflower oil is highest in polyunsaturated fat, and olive oil is highest in monounsaturated fat. Grapeseed oil has the highest smoke point, allowing it to heat well, while olive oil has the lowest.

oven spring: The rapid expansion of bread dough in the first few minutes of baking, caused by the increased temperature, and stopped when the heat reaches the point at which it kills the yeast cells. Up to a third of a bread's final volume can be added during this time.

pâte fermentée: A French pre-ferment, started 6 to 9 hours ahead of use.

peel: The paddle used to transfer bread into and out of the oven. It is usually wooden—essentially a flat, edgeless tray with a long handle.

poolish: A Polish pre-ferment, made of flour, water, and yeast, that is quite liquid. It is fermented at room temperature for up to 14 hours.

pre-ferment: A portion of dough mixed ahead of time and allowed to ferment. It is a leavening agent, and its fermentation time allows it to develop a flavour that impacts the final product.

proofing: The professional's term for the rising that happens after a dough is in its final shape—a loaf in its pan, a boule in its basket—but before baking.

Pullman: Bread baked in a loaf pan—so named because it looks a little bit like a rail car.

resting (or benching, or intermediate proofing): The period after a quantity of dough has been cut into loaf-size portions and rounded, when it is left to relax before being shaped. This is the second-last rising of the dough, the last being proofing, after the dough is shaped.

retarding: Refrigerating yeast or pre-ferment dough to slow down the fermentation or proofing. The bread takes on more of the fermented flavour the longer it is retarded.

rock salt: Salt from underground deposits left by ancient seas, which may contain impurities that have to be removed before it is used for cooking.

rounding: After dough has been cut into loaf-sized portions, the cut sides are folded into the dough in a free-form shape. This keeps the dough from drying out while it is benching, and prevents the gasses released by the yeast from escaping. After the dough has rested, this round edge helps it to spread evenly when it is being shaped.

salt: (See iodized salt, kosher salt, rock salt, sea salt, and table salt)

sautéing: Cooking food over very hot, direct heat in a small amount of fat in a pan. The difference between sautéing and frying is that sautéing is very quick.

searing: Cooking meat briefly over a high heat before turning down the heat for the balance of the cooking time. This will seal in the juices and generally improve the flavour of the end product.

sea salt: Salt is formed by evaporation of sea water. Because it has not been in the ground for eons, it is often purer than rock salt, and prized by connoisseurs.

slashes: Cuts made in an unbaked loaf before it goes into the oven. In addition to making the bread look nice, they provide an escape for excess gasses released during the baking; without them, the bread's crust would tear randomly.

soft or cake flour: Flour milled from wheats that have a relatively low protein content, therefore well suited to cakes and other baked goods with a delicate texture.

sour starter: A natural pre-ferment made without commercial yeast. Flour and water are allowed to ferment for several days to develop yeasts of their own. Dried or fresh fruit may be mixed in for their yeasts to activate the starter. More flour and water are then added until the starter is strong enough to leaven bread. This method of fermentation imparts a sour flavor that can be clearly tasted in the final "sourdough" bread.

sponge: Another type of pre-ferment, in which the yeast, some of the flour, and all the liquid called for in the recipe are mixed together and allowed to ferment for several hours before the rest of the dry ingredients are added to the dough.

table salt: Salt that has been processed to make it resistant to humidity. The cubical shape of the crystals allows them to flow better from salt shakers.

turning: A method used by most professional bakers in place of the home baker's "punching down the dough." The risen dough is turned out of its fermentation bowl, spread gently, and folded into a neat package before being returned, smooth-side up, to the fermentation bowl. Turning the dough and letting it rise again will make it stronger.

whipped butter: Butter with air incorporated into it through whipping, making it much more spreadable and increasing its volume by about 25 percent. If you are using whipped butter in a recipe, increase the volume of butter called for by about one-third.

whipping: Beating wet ingredients vigorously so as to trap air within them, making them light and fluffy.

whisking: A gentler version of whipping, generally using a hand-held whisk and stopping when the ingredients are just beginning to foam.

whole grain flours: Flours that include the grain's germ and bran as well as its endosperm. The germ of any grain contains unsaturated fat, which can cause whole grain flours to go rancid if stored unrefrigerated or for long periods of time.

yeast: (See active dry yeast, compressed yeast, and instant yeast)

Bibliography

Allen, Brigid, ed. *Food: An Oxford Anthology.* Oxford: Oxford University Press, 1994.

Applebaum, Elizabeth. www.clevelandjewish news.com/articles/2003/08/01/news/ local/ice0801.txt.

Brown, Deni. *The Royal Horticultural Society New Encyclopedia of Herbs & Their Uses.* Rev. 2002. London: DK Publishing, 1995.

Calder, Michael, and Debby Roth, eds. *Eat These Words.* New York: Calder Books, 1991.

Clevely, Andi, and Katherine Richmond. *The Complete Book of Herbs.* Toronto: Read On Publications, 1995.

Cucina Italiana. www.cucinait.com/World HomeWe.asp.

Eat, Drink, and Be Merry. Everyman's Library Pocket Poets.

Escoffier, Auguste. *The Complete Guide to the Art of Modern Cookery.* Trans. H.L. Cracknell and R.J. Kaufmann. London: Heinemann, 1979.

Fant, Maureen B., and Howard M. Isaacs. *Dictionary of Italian Cuisine.* New Jersey: ECCO Press, 1998.

Herbst, Sharon Tyler. *The New Food Lover's Companion.* Hauppauge, New York: Barron's Educational Series, 1995.

Jenkins, Steven. *The Cheese Primer.* New York: Workman Publishing, 1996.

Margen, Sheldon, and the editors of the UC Berkeley Wellness Letter. *Wellness Foods A to Z.* New York: Rebus, 2002.

Mariani, John. *The Dictionary of Italian Food and Drink.* New York: Broadway Books, 1998.

Masui, Kazuko, and Tomoko Yamada. *French Cheeses.* London: DK Publishing, 1996.

McCalman, Max, and David Gibbons. *Cheese: A Connoisseur's Guide to the World's Best.* New York: Clarkson Potter, 2005.

McGee, Harold. *On Food and Cooking: The Science and Lore of the Kitchen.* Rev. 2004. New York: Scribner, 1984.

Montagné, Prosper. *The New Larousse Gastronomique.* Trans. Marion Hunter. New York: Crown Publishers, 1977.

Morgen, Sheldon, M.D. *Wellness Foods A–Z.* New York: Rebus, 2002.

Morton, Mark. *Cupboard Love: A Dictionary of Culinary Curiosities.* 2nd rev. ed. Toronto: Insomniac Press, 2004.

Norman, Jill. *Herbs and Spices.* New York: DK Publishing, 2002.

Olver, Lynne. www.foodtimeline.org/ foodpuddings.html, 2006.

Robbins, Mary Polushkin, ed. *The Cook's Quotation Book.* New York: Penguin Books, 1984.

Rowinski, Kate, ed. *The Quotable Cook.* New York: The Lyons Press, 2000.

Stradley, Linda. www.whatscookingamerica .net/History/SaladHistory.htm. 2004.

Vanilla Enchantment. www.kitchenproject .com/vanilla/history.htm, 2004.

Washington, Peter, ed. *Eat, Drink and Be Merry.* New York: Alfred A. Knopf, 2003.

Wikipedia. www.wikipedia.org.

Index

About the Author

Linda Haynes

Linda Haynes is the co-founder of ACE Bakery and the award-winning author of the bestseller, *The ACE Bakery Cookbook*. Established in 1993, ACE Bakery is an artisan bakery providing fresh and partially baked breads to hundreds of customers across Canada, New York State, the Midwest U.S.A., and the Bahamas.

Linda was an accomplished home chef by the time her husband, Martin Connell, decided to bake bread as a weekend hobby in 1985. While traveling in France, they observed village bakers at work and slowly refined their baking skills at home in Canada. After Martin built a wood-burning bakehouse at their country retreat, Linda pinpointed the lack of artisan bakeries as a gap in the local market, and they opened ACE Bakery in 1993. In 1997, they expanded into a larger facility, and in 2000 opened an on-site bread store and café.

Linda studied journalism and worked as an ad copywriter, interviewer, and producer before turning her attention to food. She is a member of the International Association of Culinary Professionals and the Women's Culinary Network. She and Martin founded Calmeadow, an organization that supports the provision of credit and financial services to micro-entrepreneurs in developing countries who are unable to access traditional sources.

A percentage of ACE Bakery's pre-tax profits is donated to food and nutrition programs that assist low-income members of the community, to culinary scholarships, and to organic farming initiatives. All royalties from *The ACE Bakery Cookbook* were given to organizations in support of these initiatives. ACE Bakery contributes to over 100 fundraisers annually, and Linda's recipes have appeared in the *Eat to the Beat* and *Great Soup, Empty Bowls* cookbooks and in numerous newspapers across Canada.

Linda has been honoured with the International Association of Culinary Professionals Award for Philanthropy with her husband, Martin, the CESO Award for International Development, the Chief Barker Award from the Variety Club, the Entrepreneur of the Year from Ernst & Young, Canadian Business magazine, and was chosen as one of the Canadian Women Who Make a Difference in the business category. In 2006, she was awarded the Order of Canada in the field of philanthropy. The Order of Canada, Canada's highest civilian honour, recognizes a lifetime of outstanding dedication to the community and service to the nation.

Linda lives in Toronto and is currently writing a cookbook with her daughter, Devin. She enjoys skiing, reading, afternoon movies, travel, and sampling the culinary creations of her two grown children, Devin and Luke.

All royalties from *More from ACE Bakery* will be donated to organizations that work with women and children in crisis.